Giuseppe Baretti

A Journey From London to Genoa

Through England, Portugal, Spain, and France. Vol. 1

Giuseppe Baretti

A Journey From London to Genoa
Through England, Portugal, Spain, and France. Vol. 1

ISBN/EAN: 9783337128241

Printed in Europe, USA, Canada, Australia, Japan

Cover: Foto ©Andreas Hilbeck / pixelio.de

More available books at **www.hansebooks.com**

A

JOURNEY

FROM

LONDON to GENOA,

THROUGH

ENGLAND, PORTUGAL, SPAIN,

and FRANCE.

By JOSEPH BARETTI,

Secretary for Foreign Correspondence to the Royal Academy of Painting, Sculpture, and Architecture.

IN FOUR VOLUMES.

VOL. I.

LONDON,

Printed for T. DAVIES, in Ruffel-Street, Covent-Garden; and L. DAVIS, in Holborn.

MDCCLXX.

TO THE

PRESIDENT

AND

MEMBERS

OF THE

ROYAL ACADEMY

OF

PAINTING, SCULPTURE,
and ARCHITECTURE.

GENTLEMEN,

IN my various rambles through various countries, I have neither seen nor heard of a set of artists comparable to that which your monarch assembled when he formed you into an academy. Instead of attempting to express my

grati-

DEDICATION.

gratitude to that royal goodness, which has deigned to connect me with so respectable a society, I will revere and love it in silence, and endeavour to show that I deserve what it has bestowed, by a vigorous exertion of my abilities whenever occasion shall call them into your service. In the mean while, gentlemen, give me leave to dedicate to you the first work I have prepared for publication since I had the honour of belonging to you. You have a right to this small token of an affection, which inclination as well as duty has kindled in the breast of

Your most humble

and most

devoted servant,

JOSEPH BARETTI.

PREFACE.

I Have not a better apology to offer for my confidence in presenting this enlightened nation with these volumes, than that the accounts of Spain hitherto published in the English language, are in general adjudged to be very imperfect. This observation, which I had often heard repeated by many Englishmen of distinguished knowledge, has emboldened me to publish my remarks upon that country.

In the descriptions that follow, I hope it will appear that I have spared no pains to carry my reader in some measure along with me; to make him see what I saw, hear what I heard, feel what I felt, and even think and fancy whatever I thought and

and fancied myself. Should this method prove agreeable, and procure the honour of a favourable reception to my work, I shall owe it in a great part to my most revered friend Dr. Samuel Johnson, who suggested it to me, just as I was setting out on my first journey to Spain. It was he that exhorted me to write daily, and with all possible minuteness: it was he that pointed out the topics which would most interest and most delight in a future publication. To his injunctions I have kept as close as I was able, and my only fear upon this occasion, is, that some want of dexterity in the management of my narratives may justly have subjected me to the charge of egotism, as I am convinced that I have passed too frequently from my subject to myself, and made myself as much too often the hero of my own story. Yet this fear is not so predominant, as to exclude the hope that such an impropriety will be overlooked if I have but succeeded in the main point, and effectually assisted the imagination of my reader to form an idea tolerably just of Spain.

by

by exhibiting as well the face of the country, as the manners of the inhabitants. This it will appear that I have laboured pretty hard to attain; and as this is the chief end of a traveller's narrative, the real critick will not be displeased that it has been principally pursued, that subordinate and incidental parts have been less diligently considered, and that, where attention was most required, it has been most liberally bestowed.

LETTER I.

Notice given of the departure.

London, Aug. 13, 1760.

DEAR BROTHERS,

TO-morrow I shall at last quit this metropolis, and set out for Falmouth on my way home through Portugal, Spain, and the southern part of France. A long round-about way! But you know that all communication is stopped between Dover and Calais because of the war; and since I must go a long journey, I care not how long I make it. I go through Portugal and Spain rather than Holland, because of Holland I have heard and read enough, whereas I know little of Portugal and less of Spain, as there are but very imperfect accounts of either. Besides, that going the Falmouth-way, I shall likewise see the western part of this kingdom, which I have not visited.

To-morrow then is the day, from which I reckon that in about two months, or three at most, I shall have the inexpressible pleasure of seeing you again, after an absence of full ten years. My blood runs warmer and my heart beats quicker, when I think that after so long a separation I am going to sit down again to a domestic meal with one of my brothers fronting me, and one at each side of me!

Now therefore, England, farewell! I quit thee with less regret, because I am returning to my native country after a very long absence, considering the shortness of life. Yet I cannot leave thee without tears. May Heaven guard and prosper thee, thou illustrious mother of polite men and virtuous women! Thou great

great mart of literature! Thou nursery of invincible soldiers, of bold navigators, and ingenious artists, farewell, farewell! I have now forgotten all the crosses and anxieties I have undergone in thy regions for the space of ten years: but never will I forget those many amongst thy sons who have assisted me in my wants, encouraged me in my difficulties, comforted me in my adversities, and imparted to me the light of their knowledge in the dark and intricate mazes of life! Farewell, imperial England, farewell, farewell!

LETTER II.

People in the stage-coach. Salisbury and its cathedral. Militia. Bone-lace and Ducking-stool at Honiton. Love whence arising.

Exeter, Aug. 16, 1760.

BEHOLD! I am distant from London a hundred and sixty miles, and more!

On Friday I set out in one of those numberless coaches that are continually going backwards and forwards from town to town. The coach contained six people; and all six proved agreeable company to each other, though collected by mere chance: three women on one side, and three men over against them.

This begins to look like a novel; and yet it is no novel at all. In this coach were an elderly aunt with her two nieces, an English gentleman, a Scotch officer, and your eldest brother. The six horses went on at a great rate. I knew the officer's country by his pronunciation, as well as by his earnest talking with the aunt about nobility. This was his favourite topick. But the Englishman and I, employed our time to better purpose, chatting as fast as we could with the nieces, both modestly talkative and modestly pretty. Yet the good aunt was not so deep sunk into genealogy as her partner would have her; but turned to us us from time to time, and encouraged her girls to be chearful and sing songs, which they often did in such a manner, as to please even an Italian.

So agreeable a company I shall probably not find in the remainder of my journey, as it is but seldom that poor travellers are so lucky as to meet with such good-natured aunts, and with girls so pretty, so sprightly, and so obliging. The Scotchman, though somewhat stiff and ridiculous with his accounts of the great nobility in Argyleshire, yet was not unwelcome, as he is a man of very good sense in other respects. The English gentleman is learned beyond his age, and rather over-civil, as he has but lately quitted the college.

On the first day I saw nothing, as one may say, because we trotted along very fast. I could only observe that the inns, where we alighted to change horses and refresh ourselves, are all neat and good, as all inns are on all great roads in England.

land. We croffed Salifbury in hafte on the fecond day: but as I had heard much of its cathedral, I chofe to give a look at it. So I alighted, and ran like a fury through the town. Thus running I took notice of the market, which is fpacious and plentifully ftored with meat and all forts of vegetables. Along the large ftreet I croffed, there is water running on both fides juft by the houfes; which muft be a great convenience to the inhabitants. I entered the cathedral for a minute. It is a ftately building, and much more gothic than that of Milan; but not half fo large, as far as I can remember. That of Milan I take to be the largeft edifice of the kind in the whole world.

On a wide plain, not far from Salifbury, there is that thing (I know not what name to give it) called Stone-henge. I fhould be forry if you had not preferved all my former defcriptions of feveral remarkable things in this kingdom. Were
I never

I never to come to England again, as may easily be the case, I shall be very glad to have those descriptions, in order to revive a pleasing remembrance from time to time. A poor pleasure, compared to that I should feel in seeing this country again! But still, better little than nothing.

Not far from Salisbury there is likewise a country-seat belonging to an English earl, where there is the amplest collection of statues, busts, and other ancient monuments in this kingdom together with many fine paintings; almost every thing brought at an immense expence from your side of the Alps. I do not know what possessed me, that I never went to see that seat in the space of ten years, especially as I was twice in its neighbourhood. But men are naturally procrastinators: they put it off till next day, till next week; and the next day or the next week never comes.

On the third day we dined at a little town called Honiton, where they make a good deal of that lace so much admired by Italian ladies, that goes with us by the name of *Merletti d'Inghilterra*. I wonder why it is not made every where, as those who make it are neither philosophers nor conjurers, but poor ignorant women. I would have bought some for some people at Turin: but forbore, to avoid being plagued at the many custom-houses where I shall be searched before I reach home.

At Honiton, from the window of the inn, I saw a battalion of militia newly raised. They went through their military exercise; and I own I did not much admire their movements. However, they will drive the world before them when they come to be better modelled; and the French will find it no jest, if ever they dare to come over in their flat-bottom boats, and set their feet

on

on the British shore, as they have been threatening this long while.

We dined hastily. Then the Englishman and I walked out of the town, just to stretch our legs a little. We went so far as a small rivulet, where I took notice of an engine called a Ducking-stool. What is it? I will tell you if I can. It is a stool to sit on. A kind of armed wooden chair, fixed on the extremity of a pole about fifteen feet long. The pole is horizontally placed on a post just by the water, and loosely pegg'd to that post; so that by raising it at one end, you lower the stool down into the midst of the rivulet. Do you comprehend me? That stool serves at present to duck scolds and termagants: but it is said, that the superstitious inhabitants of Honiton used formerly to place on it those old women whom they thought to be witches, and duck'd them unmercifully several times; sometimes to death.

While

While the young gentleman and I were gravely philosophising on the notion of witches, which has been so general at all times and in all countries, the coach overtook us. But instead of getting into it, we wanted to pull the young ladies out of it, and give them a plunge or two, because in our days the opinion prevails, that all pretty girls are witches, and old women are so no more. Indeed Miss Anne and Miss Helen had a fine escape, and may thank the coachman who was in haste, or they had paid for their bewitching looks.

Not far from Honiton they left us as well as the Scotch officer, and the separation seemed grievous to us all. We kissed and parted; and not with eyes perfectly dry. Did I say kissed? Yes, upon my word. But you Italians make so much of a kiss, that there is no enduring you. Here we make nothing of it, especially on such occasions; nor is there any harm in it, whatever you may think.

think. What have you to say, you people on the other side of that huge mountain? I am sure I shall not abide your silly fashions, now I am used to those of England. What a ridiculous thing is kissing men and men, or women and women! The English have twenty times more wit than you. When I am amongst you again, I will positively follow the English fashions: and so, tell all the damsels in your neighbourhood, that I am coming to mend their manners. I will set up as a reformer now I am a travell'd man, and will do as all travell'd men do, when they get back home. They look, and with good reason, upon themselves as a good deal the wiser for having seen the world.

However, I felt more pain than I will tell you in the act of quitting those two amiable maidens. Perhaps I have seen them for the last time, and that is always an ugly thought! Nothing endears people so fast to each other as travelling

together

together in the same vehicle; and the effect is natural. Our love for persons arises from the pleasure we receive from them. The more pleasure they can give us, the greater our love. This is philosophy, or I am a blockhead. In that coach none of us could receive any pleasure but what was got from one of the other five; and each endeavoured to give some, that he might receive some. Thus one sung a song, one told a story, one produced a pun, one did this, and another did that. The whole world was without the coach, and within there was nothing but ourselves. Therefore having nothing else to love, we loved each other very fast. It has been observed, that the strongest love is that contracted in a jail; and the coach was for three days a perfect jail to us: so we were all become friends enough to grieve at parting. But what signifies talking? We parted, and there is an end; such transitory joys and pains are the lot of travellers.

travellers. The coach goes no further than this town, and I muft think tomorrow of another vehicle.

LETTER III.

Fine dreſſing not blameable. Fifty broken noſes. A promiſe to write trifles.

Exeter ſtill, Aug. 17, 1760.

THIS morning early I walked all over this town. It is none of the fineſt, very ill paved, and very dirty, tho' it is ſummer. In winter it muſt be ten times worſe. The houſes are generally built in ſuch a ſtyle of architecture, that Palladio would have hang'd himſelf for vexation, if he had ſeen them. I went to give a look to the cathedral. As it is Sunday, it was full of people, and the parſon was preaching againſt the vanity of dreſſing. What he ſaid upon the ſubject was ſenſible enough, and feelingly delivered; but not much to the purpoſe,

pose, as I thought, because the Exonians do not pique themselves (those at least who formed his audience) on the magnificence of their apparel. Many looked clean; but not one gaudy. Yet, had they even been fine, I do not like to hear dressing much condemned. Dressing is one of the many things that encrease the difference between the reasonable animal and the unreasonable; and any thing, be it ever so small, that increases that difference, is never much amiss. Extremes to be sure are extremes; and the vanity of dressing may be carried so far as to be ridiculous; yet sinful it can scarcely ever be: therefore, if I were a preacher, I would never bear hard upon this point, because I have observed that people well dressed, have in general a kind of respect for themselves; and whoever respects himself, does a very good thing. As for my part, I love dressing so well, that if I could afford it, it, I would be half a beau all the year round.

This cathedral is Gothic, like that of Salisbury; but much inferior to it in many respects. It is large enough for the town, but has nothing very remarkable, except the fifty figures (if I have counted them right) which adorn its front. They are alto-relievos, and all noseless. Time has pick'd off their noses, and made dust of them, as it does of all noses, whether marble or not. From the top of the church, where I ascended by a winding stair-case, the steps of which are in bad order, I have taken a view of the country round. It is very fine, full of small hills covered with trees, and watered by many streams.

Before the cathedral are some trees planted in rows, each tree fantastically cut in the form of a fan. About the walls of a ruined castle, which stands higher than the town, there is a fine walk much frequented by women, as I could see towards the latter part of the afternoon.

afternoon. I saw few men there. The prospect facing the castle on the side of the walk, is one of the most pleasing.

To-morrow my trunk will be forwarded to Falmouth in a cart or waggon. The English gentleman and I go to Plymouth, where I intend to make but a short stay. I want to be at Falmouth and embark for Lisbon. Having no more pretty girls to travel with, I find that I grow impatient, and long to see my journey's end, thinking more and more deeply on the three thousand miles I have to go. It is the seventh or eighth part of the globe's circumference! From Plymouth, and even from Falmouth, I will write to you again, and send my letters back to London, that they may be forwarded to you from thence. From Falmouth onward I propose to write to you every night, even when I am at sea, and tell you the story of every day. But whatever I write, as I go on, shall not be brought to you by any body but myself.

Be

Be sure I will write a world of things that I shall see or hear. Trifles indeed they will commonly be, as I shall have no leisure any where to make deep remarks. Yet I will endeavour to be entertaining, at least to myself; as I shall probably have no other means of beguiling the evenings but by my quill.

LETTER IV.

Manufactures of Serges and Tapestry. Father Norbert and his workmen from France.

Plymouth, Aug. 18, 1760.

I Left Exeter this morning at eleven, after having visited two manufactories, one of serges, and the other of that sort of tapestry, which in French is called *Gobelins* from the place where it is made at Paris. The serges of Exeter are, as I am told, chiefly exported into Catholic-countries for the use of monks and nuns of various orders. In several storehouses of that town there are so many bales of it, as would suffice to make an intrenchment round the camp of the Austrians, who are said to be so numerous in Saxony. I mean that at Exeter they make a large quantity of those serges: but travellers must exaggerate if they will prove entertaining. Many fanatical speculators would fain see all our religious orders abolished: but, were it not for those other fanaticks who compose those orders, Exeter would fare but poorly.

As to the Gobelin-tapestry, the art of making it in perfection was introduced in England by a famous anti-jesuit, the reverend father Norbert, a French capuchin-friar, whom Benedict XIV (a kind of anti-jesuit himself) permitted to go and live in England, on condition he should play the missionary there, and convert the good people to his church. But, instead of doing as he was bid, and as he had promised, the honest fellow took the liberty of secularising himself,

assumed

aſſumed the name of Monſieur Pariſot, and turned director of a manufactory of that ſort of tapeſtry. In this undertaking he found means of being aſſiſted by a voluntary ſubſcription of the Engliſh nobility and gentry, which amounted to more than ten thouſand pounds, as I was told at that time. That ſubſcription the Monſieur pocketted ſoon after his arrival in London. I went ſeveral times from London to Fulham to ſee his looms, which would have procured him a pretty livelihood if he had been a man of ſome economy. But he lived at ſuch a rate, and was poſſeſſed of ſo many virtues, eſpecially thoſe two cardinal ones vulgarly called luſt and vanity, that he contracted many debts in a little time, turned bankrupt, and ran away.

The looms and other manufacturing implements which he could not carry off, were ſold by auction; and one Mr. Paſſavan bought them for little more than nothing.

nothing. With them he set up a diminutive manufactory at Exeter, after having taken into his service a few deserters from the Gobelins of Paris, who were inticed away by the friar's magnificent promises. These workmen, in consequence of those promises, came over to England, fairly venturing a halter, if they had been caught in the act of deserting. But the friar was far from keeping his word with them as soon as he had a sufficient number of them in his power. The salaries he then appointed them (and they were forced to accept) were but scanty. On his running away from England, the poor fellows found themselves in a very sad plight. They knew no other trade but that of tapestry-making, were ignorant of the language, and could not go back to France, where they would have been hanged for their desertion. Mr. Passavan picked out of the streets of London those few whom hunger and wretchedness had not time

to

to kill, and got them to Exeter, where he makes a penny out of their labour.

One part of this ſtory I knew ſome years ago: the other I had from thoſe few Frenchmen at Exeter; and I fancy you will not be difpleaſed with this anecdote of a man ſo much talked of in Italy for his virulent writings againſt the Jeſuits; whoſe books were for a time in every body's hands; and whoſe character proved at laſt no better than thoſe of the worſt part amongſt thoſe whom he cenſured.

I take now my leave of Exeter and of the organ of its cathedral, which the Exonians ſcruple not to ſay is the fineſt in England. And now you muſt fancy that you ſee me in a poſt-chaiſe haſtening to Plymouth, quite enamoured with the rural beauties of Devonſhire, which are not inferiour to the beſt parts of Piedmont and Lombardy. At night I reached this town with a whole neck. A lucky thing enough, conſidering how precipitoufly the poftillions drove. It was quite dark when I alighted at the inn. I have written thefe lines while fupper is making ready. Can any body fay that I am idle?

LETTER V.

A man of war and a dock vifited.

Plymouth ftill, Aug. 19, 1760.

THIS morning I rambled about this fmall and irregular town, and vifited its two churches, called St. Andrew and St. Charles. The Englifh care but little for faints: yet they give their names to churches. A little piece of incongruity, as I take it. It proves how difficult it is to get rid of ancient cuftoms.

I walked a while on the key of the harbour and along the fea-fhore, where I faw nothing very remarkable, excepting two bay-mules. One of them was lame. And here, to keep up the character of a fkilful, attentive, and judicious traveller, I muft

I must tell you that mules in England are far from being so common as with us. These two are almost all that I have seen in ten years.

Having noted down the lame mule in my memorandum-book with a pencil, I went towards the arsenal, or dock, as they call it here. It is about two miles distant from the town. In my way there, and just by it, I spy'd a man of war of sixty or seventy guns, called the Nottingham. They were refitting it, being just come from a long voyage. As I had never seen the inside of a man of war, I chose to visit it thoroughly with the assistance of two sailors, who explained to me the use of every thing in it, answering my numerous and foolish questions with a great deal of patience. What is this, and what is that, and what is the use of that other thing? Indeed the fellows were much in the right if they laughed at my ignorance of every thing. I am sure they winked at each other, and

looked

looked arch: yet I say it again, they were perfectly right to make sport of such a mere landman as I am.

This visit lasted little less than three hours. But, just as it was over, and I was taking my leave of my friendly instructors, a sun-burnt sort of a gentleman came on board; one of the under-officers, I think. He approached me with a very particular kind of civility; something of openness mixed with roughness. Indeed I know not what name to give to that kind of civility. A medley of boldness, contempt, self-sufficiency, and kindness. Extract an idea out of these different ideas, and enjoy it. Hearing I was a stranger who had never been before under the deck of a war-ship, he took hold at once of both my hands, and grasped them so tenaciously, that I could not escape him. " *Here, Sir, let's walk below,* " *and I'll show her to you. A damn'd old* " *baggage she; and we'll all go to the bottom* " *in her next voyage; but I don't care a* " *rush.*"

"*rush.*" It was with the utmost difficulty I saved myself from his well-meant kindness. I entered an inn in the dock, and dined.

After dinner I went in search of an engineer for whom I had a letter, in which he was desired by a friend in London to show me the dock and any other thing curious about Plymouth. He is a most gentleman-like man, and possessed of much polite learning besides his skill in his profession.

He took me into the most hidden recesses of the dock, and showed me every thing. There I saw great heaps of cannon and mountains of cannon-balls, impatiently waiting for an opportunity to assist in the propagation of the human species : there I saw numberless masts of various sizes, all modestly lying down in a vast close : there I saw a prodigious long room, in which many men, running with their backs forwards and their bellies
backwards,

backwards, (you comprehend me) were making those ropes, which are afterwards joined many together, and formed into cables as big as my waist. There I saw the vast chauldrons full of tar, where those ropes are boiled: and there I saw a very large wheel so constructed, that it contains about a dozen men in itself, who make it turn with great velocity by their incessant trampling upon some wooden bars that are laid across its inside. You have seen what we call a winding-cage put in motion by the bird it contains? That wheel is made upon the principles of a winding-cage, and those men in it may be called the bird. They had no more cloaths on than a frog, excepting their trowsers. The men turn the wheel; the wheel moves a press; the press squeezes the ropes that have been boiled in the chauldrons; and the ropes thus squeezed, emit the tar with which they were there impregnated. In short, I saw so many things in that dock, that Briareus, who
had

had fifty writing-hands out of his hundred, would not be able to set them all down in an age, were he charged with making the inventory. Upon my credit, as I came out of that place I was little less than stupified. My faculties were nearly overpowered by the immense variety of objects that had past before my eyes. It was dark when I got back to the inn.

LETTER VI.

Fortifications. Mount Edgecombe. An habitation fit for Jean-Jacques. *An antiquarian and his daughter.*

Plymouth still, Aug. 20, 1760.

THE courteous engineer called upon me this morning early, and took me into a barge rowed by six stout fellows, besides the man at the rudder. We crossed with great swiftness a part of the harbour, and landed on a small rocky islet, called St. Nicholas, which has been placed

placed by nature in the very mouth of Plymouth-harbour. In lefs than half an hour we made the tour of the fortification upon it. Then we went to fee the citadel, which is certainly very ftrong, and fo well provided with batteries, that woe to the French Argonaut who fhould ever dare to come in fearch of the golden fleece on this fhore. Yet I was not aftonifhed at its ftrength. He who has feen our fortreffes on the Alps, efpecially *Feneftrelles* and *La Brunette*, needs not to be furprifed at any thing of that kind.

It was Charles the Second who built this citadel, in order to bridle the inhabitants of Plymouth, who had fided with Cromwell in the famous civil war. For thefe feveral years paft they have been adding new fortifications to the harbour and the dock. So that, if the Plymouth-people had once the mortification to fee themfelves checked by them, they have now the pleafure to fee themfelves fecured againft all foreign invaders. No foe
muft

must now think of landing there without an immense force. I even question whether it would be possible for any force to take it (I mean any force the French can muster) considering how the approach to it is rendered difficult by St. Nicholas and the citadel mutually supporting each other. Be it possible or not, I should not be pleased to be in the head-ship that came on so desperate an errand.

After dinner we got again into the barge, and made towards a hill about as high as that of the capuchins on the right side of your Po. They call it Mount-Edgecombe; and it is, properly speaking, a promontory which juts out into the sea on the right side of Plymouth-harbour. The proprietor of it is an English lord, who has a house upon it. In the whole world there is perhaps not another so well situated. A bold expression, you will say. But were you to see it, you would be astonished at the prospect it commands.

From its windows, and indeed from that whole side of the hill, you see straight afore you the vast ocean extending itself beyond the reach of eyes. The immense liquid plain has its uniformity interrupted only in one small place about ten miles from the land. I mean, that about ten miles off at sea there is a Light-house erected on a rock, which stands absolutely by itself, and is called *The Eddy-stone*. The Light-house is very visible from Mount-Edgecombe, though at such a distance. On your left hand you have the harbour with the islet of St. Nicholas, the citadel, the dock, and the town of Plymouth. The harbour swarms with men of war and ships of several sizes, some at anchor and some in motion, and with numberless boats perpetually rowing or sailing backwards and forwards; the whole of this surrounded by a vast tract of fine country, diversified by a great many hills and streams of water. Add to this, that under the windows and all about the park, there are cows, and deer, and geese, and turkeys, and other animals peaceably feeding upon a verdant carpet bounded all round by a circular walk. A fine contrast to the busy scene transacted below in the harbour.

What do you say to it now? They speak of the Chartreuse at Naples, and they say it is the finest situation in the world. I believe it. But Mount-Edgecombe is also the finest; and so you have two finest, one at Naples, and the other in Devonshire. In Queen Elizabeth's time the admiral of the Spanish Armada, making sure of conquering this kingdom, begg'd Mount-Edgecombe of Philip II by way of reward for his intended conquest. Philip promised to give it; but the English admiral hindered him from keeping his promise, by accomplishing the destruction of the Armada with his invention of fire-ships. A horrible storm had already begun that destruction.

Of the Light-houſe and rock on which it ſtands, I ſaw once the model in London. There was formerly another light-houſe on that rock, which was waſhed away by the ſea on a ſtormy night, and ſtill another that was accidentally burnt. I remember very well that I admired much the model of this. The ingenuity of the architect (one Mr. Smeaton) was great, who found the means of erecting ſuch an edifice in ſuch a place; that is, upon a ſloping rock perfectly naked, and almoſt inceſſantly beaten by millions of the moſt tremendous waves.

To think of digging that rock, and thus give the edifice a good foundation, was utterly impoſſible, as the rock is near as hard as porphyry. The architect therefore had a multitude of holes bored into it, and large iron bars driven into thoſe holes. To bore ſuch holes required no ſmall labour, as you may imagine. Then, between bar and bar the foundation was laid, by connecting large flat ſtones in
ſuch

such a manner, that each entered into a part of the next. No sand was employed there but what was fetched so far as the neighbourhood of Rome. You know the nature of the *Pozzolana*, that hardens under water every day more when mixed with lime, and incorporates with the stones in such a manner, as to make one solid mass with them in a little time.

This was certainly a noble undertaking; and thus the dangerous rock is made visible to nocturnal navigators, as lights are shown every night on the top of that strange edifice by two men, who live constantly there, and sometimes see no body for whole months, especially in winter. Those men have provisions sent them from Plymouth when the weather will permit. But let them be ever so plentifully supplied, still they must husband them with great care for fear of a long tempestuous winter, that leaves no room for sending them any thing. What a happy life some mortals lead on the surface of this globe! To be shut up in a small apartment (a very small one) on the top of a tower seventy foot high, and see nothing but water from its narrow windows, and hear no other sound but that of the raging billows incessantly beating about them! I am told that those billows are often such, as to approach the very top of the Light-house, and sprinkle its narrow windows. The celebrated Rousseau never heard of such a place, I suppose; or he would have begg'd the employ of lamp-lighter there, he who hates so much all converse with mankind. It is impossible to imagine a properer mansion for a philosopher so much out of humour with this wicked world.

After having walk'd a while in the circular walk of Mount-Edgecombe, and well considered all the parts of that surprising prospect, I took my leave of the engineer, who was going another way, and went back to the barge with another gentleman who had dined with us. His chearful

chearful countenance, the liveliness of his conversation, and the reverend hoariness of his locks, made me readily sympathise with him. He is a Naturalist and an Antiquarian. As we crossed the harbour again, he pointed at a place on the left hand, and made me take notice of some large holes which go deep under the shore. Near those holes, said he, lived in ancient days a mighty giant called *Og-magog*; and we are informed by an old chronicle, that he fought once a most terrible battle with another giant called *Corineus*, whom he killed and threw head-long into the sea just by those holes: so that they have retained the name of the victor to this day, and are called *The holes of Og-magog*.

On our landing at Plymouth the gentleman insisted upon my going to eat a bit of supper with him; and while it was making ready, he showed me his collection of medals and natural curiosities. But oh the wonderful discretion of a Naturalift and Antiquarian! He only pointed curforily to a few of the rareft pieces in the collection, and did not teize me with minute and tirefome details. Many of his brethern have got the trick of keeping you a long time, defcanting upon every rufty medal they have, upon every broken idolet, every reptile, every plant, every petrifaction, and every chryftallifation; nor are they aware, that he who has not made fuch things the principal object of his ftudies, confiders a good many of them as mere baubles, and cannot look upon them with fuch eager eyes as they do themfelves, who having employed many of their thoughts about them, and been at a great deal of trouble in collecting, hold almoft every individual piece as dear as a jewel.

Do not imagine however, that I condemn the collectors of medals; much lefs thofe of natural curiofities. He who has leifure and means, does very well to employ them this way, if he knows of no

better

better to render himſelf uſeful to the literary commonwealth. It is of conſiderable advantage in the proſecution of our ſtudies to know ſomething of ancient coins and other remains of remote ages; and it is a moſt rational ſatisfaction to be acquainted with every pebble that lies in your way, with every weed you tread upon, and with every flower you pluck up. And to be able to range almoſt every thing you ſee in its proper claſs, will certainly help on life in a manner delightful as well as innocent. But to honour accidental inſpectors with your prolix details, proves intolerably fatiguing.

My gentleman is none of theſe over-officious explainers, and did not put me out of patience for a ſingle moment. Nor will I paſs over in ſilence his daughter, who ſeemed to be very well verſed in the maidenly ſcience of ſhells and butterflies, and not even ignorant of the manner in which coral is formed and inſects live in its cavities, as I found by converſation while

while at supper. Her father has made her the keeper of his cabinet, and she knows so much of every thing in it, as to supply pretty well his absence when there is occasion to show it to strangers. I wish we had in Italy many young ladies as learned as Miss Betsey, and able to procure themselves so harmless a pastime as that of examining the various productions of nature. I think it would be a very advantageous addition to that of dancing well, and fingering a harpsichord with a masterly hand.

But the pleasure of scribbling has made me encroach upon the hour of going to bed. Therefore, good night. I see the dawn peeping out. It is near four by my watch, and rather time to set out than to go to sleep. However, I will go to sleep; and so good night again.

LET-

LETTER VII.

Petty tyranny scarcely avoidable. Incessant rain.

From an inn called Horse-bridge, Aug. 21, 1760.

THIS has proved a very rainy day, which has made my short journey very disagreeable. At the town where I dined, having nobody to talk to, and yet wanting to talk, I asked mine hostess how she went on in her business. Very poorly, said the old woman. I am sorry, said I, to hear you say so. But how can this be, as this town seems so populous?

She then informed me, that almost the whole territory of that town belongs to a noble peer of this realm, who never goes there, and leaves all his concerns to the management of an agent. The agent by these means, from a very insignificant fellow that he originally was, is become a most considerable personage in the town and plays the bashaw over almost every body

body there. Do you see (quoth the woman) that girl there? Well: she is a virtuous girl, and never would mind the agent. I will say no more: but he took something amiss of us, and declared himself our enemy. He is all-powerful here, and does right and wrong, just as he lists: nor can we get any redress, as the justice himself stands in fear of him. Some of the townsmen, who have been wronged by the agent as well as we, are gone severally to London to complain of him to the lord; but never could get admittance, because he is too great a man to be spoke to by ordinary people; besides that several of his grace's servants are in the bashaw's interest, and take care to stop all information. Every body gives a good word to the lord, and says that he would set all things to rights (*a*) if he was but apprised of what is doing in this place.

(*a*) *The complaints of the inhabitants (as I was casually apprised since my return to England) have reached the peer, and the agent has been turned out of his place.*

To

To diſtreſs me and my family, the agent will have nothing further to do with any inhabitant who comes to my inn; and he has it in his power to harraſs many, and deny bread to many, having, as I ſaid, the management of almoſt all the land in the territory, and many of them being the lord's tenants. Thus I am ruined, continued the old woman, as I have no means of ſubſiſtence but ſuch chance-travellers as you are, and the road from Plymouth to Falmouth not much frequented. Not a ſingle glaſs of cyder can I ſell to any body dependant on that man. They all avoid me and my houſe as if the plague was in it!

Now, ye Engliſhmen, ſaid I to myſelf, behold! Here as well as elſewhere, the whale ſwallows up the ſmall fiſhes, whatever you may ſay of your laws, which you think ſo very antidotal againſt all ſort of tyranny. Your laws, you ſay, are an adamantine ſhield that covers your whole iſland. No oppreſſion is here of any kind;

kind; no: not the least shadow of it. But go to mine hostess, gentlemen, and you will hear another story. You will hear that it is in your country as in all others; I mean that no such laws can be thought on by mortal legislators, as perfectly to screen the weak against the strong, or the poor against the rich; especially when the subject of complaint is not so great as to draw the public attention, which is generally the case in those many oppressions that the little endure from the great. Innumerable are the distresses that one part of mankind would heap upon the other, were it not for a law much higher than any you can pass. That law you must all endeavour to inculcate to each other, that it may spread further and further. That alone will prove powerful if you keep it: but if you despise or neglect it, none else will be much conducive to the suppression and extinction of petty tyranny.

Thus

Thus did I go on moralizing the whole afternoon, closely shut up in my chaise because of the rain. This inn of Horse-bridge is the last place in Devonshire. To-morrow I shall be in Cornwall by break of day.

LETTER VIII.

Chivalry-books. Variations of speech. Tin, Gold, and Coal-mines in Italy. Why should we work hard?

Falmouth, Aug. 22, 1760.

WITHIN pistol-shot of the house where I wrote my last, there is a brook with a plank over it. At the east-end of that plank Devonshire ends, and at the west-end Cornwall begins.

Cornwall is a province frequently mentioned in our ancient books of chivalry. It is represented as a country, where knights-errant often met with strange adventures: With distressed damsels riding about on milk-white palfreys in search of affiftance againft fome giant who had robbed them of their lovers, or againft fome necromancer who had fhut up fome beautiful queen in his enchanted tower.

 Why Cornwal was oftener named in thofe books than Devonfhire or fome other of the adjacent parts, is not eafy to fay. Perhaps fome fafhionable defcription of that country determined their choice, or perhaps in the ages of chivalry Cornwall was better known to the Italians than Devonfhire and other adjacent parts on account of the tin with which it abounds. The Italians were then the greateft (perhaps the only) navigators in Europe, and knew one better than the other upon that account. Give a better guefs if you can as to the predilection our romancers had for this province whenever they laid the fcene in Great Britain.

 As Falmouth is little lefs than three hundred miles from London, I expected to be much puzzled in many parts by variation of fpeech. But I have found that

the

the same language is very nearly spoken all along the road. The very speech of Falmouth is so like that of London, as not to give me the least trouble. This would not have been the case in Italy, where in a much shorter space you meet with dialects quite unintelligible to the Tuscans or the Romans, and, what is still more surprising, with other manners and other tenours of living, which is not perceptibly the case from London to Falmouth.

However it is lucky that I happened not to come this way about a century and half ago; for I am told that a dialect of the Welch language was then spoken throughout this province, which had certainly been utterly unintelligible to me. How the Cornish came to be quite annihilated in so short a time is matter of astonishment, considering that the present inhabitants are not colonists, but lineal descendants from the inhabitants of that age.

As it has rained apace ever since I crossed the small brook above-mentioned, I could see almost nothing these three days but the road and the inns where I alighted. I cannot therefore tell you any very remarkable thing of the country which I left behind. It was my intention to stop at Truro, and go to see the tin-mines in its neighbourhood; but this untimely rain, which still continues, has defeated my scheme, and put me quite out of humour; so that I jogged along to this place, and thus have deprived both you and myself of some entertainment and information.

Truro is the chief town of Cornwall. By what I could see of it, I liked it better than either Exeter or Plymouth. Along one of the streets lie scattered a great many square pieces of tin, each of about three hundred pounds weight, as I am told. They tell me likewise, that tin is dug out of the mine along with a great deal of earth; and not in bits or lumps, but

but in grains as small as common sand. The tin is separated from the earth by several washings, and, when thus separated, is melted and cast into those square pieces. The pieces are marked with the king's stamp, and a small duty is paid for that mark. Then it is melted again, and cast into ingots about as big as my thumb, and little less than three spans long; and in this form is tin transported wherever it goes. I got one of those ingots, and could as easily bend it as I can a rope. In the bending it gives a successive cracking sound, and yet it is not a sound, properly speaking: it is rather a noise. Nor will an ingot break by bending, except you twist it hard, and contrary-wise. The square pieces look very much like silver unpolished, and emit a pretty sound or tinckling when struck with a stick or a stone.

It is a good thing for the Cornish people to have plenty of a commodity like this, which is of general use, and almost

peculiar

peculiar to their province. It makes them ample amends for their foil, which in many places feemed to me very barren. I do not know whether we have any tin in Italy : but I have once feen an Englifh book of travels (whofe title or author I cannot now recollect) in which it is faid, that the hills about Spoleto and Norcia contain much of it. If this is true, our Italians muft be confidered as lefs induftrious than the Englifh, for not fearching into thofe hills. It is a remark made by many foreigners, that if nature does not place her treafures within the reach of our countrymen, they fcarcely deign to have recourfe to art in order to get at them. I will not for the prefent attempt to fettle the ballance of induftry between ours and other nations. Such a difcuffion would be endlefs. This however I will fay, that we have coal-mines in feveral parts of Italy, which were never looked into, but by fome curious naturalifts; and that I have myfelf feen hundreds

dreds of poor people searching for gold in some of our rivers, particularly after a heavy shower in a torrent called *Orba*, which runs between the high Monferrat and the Genoese; and was told, that many a one is often so lucky, as to get in a few hours as much of it as will sell for a crown and more. Yet no body ever made the least attempt towards discovering the place from which that gold is washed down.

These and several other neglects of this nature, have often been censured by strangers, and the character of the Italians for industry is not so great in foreign countries as it ought perhaps to be. But though we do not search for coals and metals, yet I cannot find in my heart peevishness enough to join with these censurers. It is true that to be rich is a most convenient thing; and you will easily believe me when I tell you, that I should not at all be displeased at an income of ten thousand pounds, and even ten thousand times

times more. But when I confider that Italy fares as well, taken all together, as any other country that can be named; that there are as few real wants amongft us as any where elfe; that very few amongft our poor live in perfect idlenefs; and that few, very few, are thofe who can ever be enriched by hard and conftant labour; when I confider all this, I cannot indeed wifh to fee labour much multiplied amongft our poor. And pray, why fhould they

Ranfack the centre, and with impious hand
Rifle the bowels of their mother earth
For treafures better hid?

and why fhould they work harder and harder, to no better purpofe than to make the rich ftill richer?

Italy has been fo favoured by providence, that it might fhift by itfelf, better perhaps than any other country, if it were put to it. We have a fertile ground that yields with moderate labour not only every neceffary of life, but even a great many

many articles of luxury; nay, we have those articles in such plenty, that we can well spare a large share for other nations, and exchange them for what we fancy will do us good. We want nothing realy, but a succession of good governors careful to see that people may have a share suitable to their several ranks of those blessings which the country yields with great liberality; and let English, Dutch, or other people, born in climates less kind than ours, perpetually contrive new schemes to load their poor with work, and think perpetually how to put them all (if it were feasible) about unbosoming mountains, or plowing the ocean in numberless directions, in order to encrease the number of the few who are to enjoy without working. Too much must be endured by those, to whose lot it falls to go upon such errands; and I like not to see our poor employed in occupations that kill some and harass many.

I know that politicians and traders have millions of things ready to offer against reasonings like this. The very dullest amongst them, thinks himself equal to the task of proving, that the Italians, because less industrious, must of course be less happy than the English or the Dutch, who are the modern patterns of industry. But let us take notice, that in the dictionary of traders and politicians, riches and happiness are made perfectly synonimous, though they are not strictly so in the lexicon of philosophers; and let us reflect above all, that it is impossible ro enrich the hundredth part of the inhabitants of any country, but through the hard and incessant labour of the other ninety nine parts.

LETTER IX.

Pilchards. Packet-boats, and laſt farewell to England.

Falmouth ſtill, One o'clock in the afternoon, Aug. 23, 1760.

MY trunk has been carried this minute on board; I have already dined; I have paid four guineas for the permiſſion of embarking; and have no further buſineſs here but to wait for the ſignal of departure. The weather is perfectly fair, and the wind as favourable as one can wiſh, ſince the ſtreamer on the maſt-head points exactly to Liſbon.

It was a moſt lucky thing that I reached Falmouth laſt night. Had I tarried four and twenty hours longer on the road, I ſhould have been obliged to paſs a week or a fortnight here, waiting for another packet; which had proved ſomewhat vexatious, as this place affords no other amuſement to an unknown stranger, but that of walking about, or looking on the sea.

Last night I supped with some gentlemen just arrived from the place where I am going. They had a very bad passage. Calms and storms alternately; and were full four and forty days about it. If this was to be my case, it would heartily make me curse my curiosity to see Portugal and Spain. However let us hope for the best. I have now advanced too far to retreat, and will take my chance.

So by and by I shall be in England no more! This is no pleasing consideration. By and by I shall be tost up and down the waves. And this other consideration, do you think it pleasing? But, what is really not pleasing, I shall have no other company on board, except the people that belong to the packet. What shall I do to employ my time if the passage proves long? Scribble and read. But a man cannot read and scribble for ever. I shall want a little talk likewise; and the

people

people of the packet, I suppose, will have other business to mind than my converse. Put all this together, and say whether my present situation can raise your envy. But it is a folly to abandon ourselves to our imaginations when they are of the gloomy kind.

I had not much rest last night, as I went to bed much vexed at the rain that continued pouring without any sort of discretion. But rising with the sun, I was mightly pleased to see it shine in its greatest glory, and not the least speck of a cloud in the whole horizon. I walked along the shore, waiting for the captain of the packet, with whom I was to go for the passport. In my walk I met with a gentleman, an early riser, it seems, as well as myself. I bowed; he bowed. Going for Lisbon, sir? Yes, sir. I hope you will have a good passage. I thank you kindly. Words beget words. We said something of the war; we made a jest of the French; praised the king of

Prussia,

Prussia, prince Ferdinand, and so forth. Then we came to talk of Falmouth. He told me that he traded much in pilchards; and that he sent every year several ship-loads to several parts of Europe, and particularly to Italy.

Pilchards, as I could collect from his discourse, are the chief commodity that the Falmouth people have for trade. The fish comes in this neighbourhood generally three times a year, and always in large shoals. That which is caught in winter proves best and sells best. They take immense quantities of it; salt it; stow it in large barrels; and sell it for the greatest part to the several catholic nations. Should the Pope turn Protestant, and abolish lent and meagre days, or only tell us that it is no sin to eat a good fowl on a Friday, the Falmouthians would have no great temptation to laugh at the jest. Yet, besides this resource, they have money necessarily circulating in the town, in consequence of the many packets

packets here stationed for several parts of the West-Indies, Spain, and Portugal. Nor is this country barren and unpleasant. I like very well what I have seen of it, and Falmouth seems to me one of those innumerable places where a man may live agreeably, provided he has wherewithal to supply all his wants. But hark! it is the signal-gun that calls me on board with its resounding voice. So farewell England, farewell again and again.

LETTER X.

Sea-sickness. Monsieur or the Dog. Neither Fight nor storm. Englishmen mending.

From on board the King-George-Packet, about a hundred and fifty miles off Falmouth. Aug. 24, 1760.

YESTERDAY about two o'clock in the afternoon I came hastily on board. The sails were spread, and in less than three hours, with the shore always in view, we found ourselves off a place called

called *Land's End*, which (as the name implies) is the western-most point of England. I fetch'd a deep sigh when a little after I saw it no more.

It was near eight when all I could see about us was nothing but water, water, water. The sky was quite bright, the wind blew very fresh, and the sea was as flat as the table I am writing upon: so that, finding I was already thirty miles from the shore without the least symptom of the sea-sickness, I made sure I should escape it. It came into my head that about five and twenty years ago, crossing that little puddle pompously called *the Adriatic Sea* by the Venetians, I was taken ill within two or three miles from the land; and that the same had happened ten years ago when I went from Boulogne to Dover. This was good ground enough for hope, considering my present distance from the shore. Yet that hope was blasted, and at sun-set my stomach wrought with such violence, that for near three hours I was more ill than words can express. I was carried down little less than senseless, and put to bed. An end was soon put to my torment by my falling into a most profound sleep, in spight of the inceffant crackings of the ship, and in spight of the walking, talking, singing, and jumping of the sailors.

It was near eight this morning when I was awakened by some of the fellows crying out *a sail, a sail*. As I found myself tolerably well, I got up instantly, and went upon deck, where about an hour after I saw through my spying-glass a ship that seemed to make towards us. Now, thought I, I shall have something to enliven my letter of to-day. Every man on board was looking at the ship; some through telescopes, and some with their own eyes. None could as yet tell whether it was a friend or a foe. This

packet

packet is a moſt ſpecial ſailer; ſo that none of our people feared being overtaken by any purſuer, and we went on as if no body had been in ſight. The captain inquired with great kindneſs after my health, hoped I would be ſick no more, and order'd tea, which was moſt acceptable, as my throat was very ſore becauſe of the efforts made laſt night. I breakfaſted heartily; then looked again at the ſhip that followed; then took up a book; then went down to dine; then went up to look at the ſhip again; then read again and again. Towards five this afternoon the ſhip was within two or three miles of us, and ſeveral of our people were poſitive that it was *Marſhal Belliſle*, a privateer of Morlaix that carries twelve or fourteen guns. By what marks they could know it, I cannot tell. As this opinion prevailed, our tars wiſhed the Dog would come an inch nearer, juſt to give him a broadſide or two, by way of

pay-

paying him for his fawcinefs in looking at us. As we have a few guns more than the Dog, (for dog is the word) we would prefently cure him of his impertinence. But packets are ftrictly forbidden to fight, when fighting can be avoided by failing away. They cannot even ftop to attack enemies of inferior force. Therefore Monfieur, or the Dog, (the two words are fynonimous) is perfectly fafe, and may follow as long as he lifts. We have now fpread a few additional fails, and the captain tells me, that in about two hours we fhall fee him no more if this wind continues. My account of this voyage therefore will not be graced with the narration of a naval combat, which would make it much prettier; and it will prove quite infipid if we are alfo fo unlucky as not to meet with a ftorm to excite a little my powers of defcription.

But what fhall I fay now the privateer has difappeared? I want a fubject for
scribbling

scribbling half an hour longer, and here I have none at hand. Let me step back to the dear island I quitted yesterday.

The farther I went from London, the more tractable seem'd the low people. None did I meet that was sparing of bows and civil behaviour; and in the whole journey I never was honoured once with the pretty appellation of *French dog*, so liberally bestowed by the London rabble upon those who have an outlandish look; and you know how few are the strangers that can look like natives any where.

This custom of abusing strangers without the least provocation, is by many attributed to the freedom of the English government: But I am far from being of this opinion, as the custom of abusing strangers is not peculiar to the English. There are other governments quite different from the British, where the low people make thus free with those who are not their countrymen; and call them

by

by injurious names as they go by. However, in the space of ten years, I have observed that the English populace have considerably mended their manners in this particular; and am persuaded that in about twenty years more they will become quite as civil to strangers as the French and the Italians. When I first went to London, I remember that a stranger could scarcely walk about with his hair in a bag without being affronted. Every porter and every street-walker would give a pull to his bag, merely to rejoice themselves and passengers: but now, both strangers and natives wear bags about London without molestation; nor is the *French-dog* by far so much in fashion as it was then, when they would even bestow it upon a Turk, whose chin was shaded by a beard, and whose head was hidden in a turban.

The low people all over the kingdom seem to think that there are but two nations in the world, the English and the French;

French; and he must be a Frenchman who is not an Englishman. Then they know something of a sea-faring people called the Dutch, for whom they have the greatest contempt. But talk to them of other nations; of the Italians for instance: They have heard something of the Italians; but a'n't the 'Talians French? What are they? Have they any bread to eat, or any beer to drink, like the English? Or do they feed upon soop-meagre and frogs like the French?

Here you will be apt to wonder at the ignorance of the English populace: but while you wonder, be pleased to recollect that our Italian populace are full as ignorant, and even more. What notions have our populace of the English? They have heard that the English do not believe the Pope to be infallible: of course they are not Christians. But what are they? No body knows for certain; but the English believe in transmigration, and that they shall be turned into some animal

animal or other after death; mean while they are all Lords, and not men and women, but something else, no body knows what.

Such are the notions our low people have of the English; and what encreases their absurdity is, that they see English travellers every day, who look as much like men as the Pope himself. And as to the English notions about eating and drinking, did you ever hear of the honest Neapolitan who was going to Rome? He put bread and onions in his post-chaise, not knowing (said he) whether there was any thing to eat at such a distance from Naples.

Excusing therefore their rudeness to strangers, and their contempt for all other countries, [into which contempt they are betray'd by many of their daily scribblers, who are incessantly reviling all other countries;] the populace of England is far from being so hateful as strangers are apt to think a little after their arrival in London. I have seen them contribute as many shillings as they could spare, towards the maintenance of the French prisoners they have made in the present war: I have seen them sorry when the news came that Damiens had stabb'd the King of France: and I have heard an universal shout of joy when their parliament voted a hundred thousand pounds to the Portuguese on hearing of the tremendous earthquake. What do you say to this? Is it possible to hate people of this make? What signifies their ridiculous custom of calling names, by which foreign blockheads are so much offended?

But 'tis time to go to bed. If I am in the humour to-morrow, I will resume this topic, and tell you more of the English. Except a little sore-throat, I now find myself better than ever I was in my life; and yet last night my sickness was so horrible, that I thought it
im-

impossible to survive it. It is really a thing that feels fatal.

LETTER XI.

Acquaintance contracted at Sea. A Bagpipe. Juno's and Venus's.

King George Packet, Aug. 25, 1760.

THE Captain's name is Bawn, and the Lieutenant's Oak. They are both very kind and very civil; nor did I ever see any people mind their business more closely than they do theirs. I think they live without sleep. They are always upon deck, and attentive to the sailors, that each may stick to his respective duty. Scarcely dare I to exchange ten words with either for fear of proving troublesome. However, when we are *alongside of a buttock of beef*, as they phrase it, we talk fast enough, and drink to each other merrily. But you do not know that I have found a treasure in this ship. Yes, in-

indeed; and this treasure is the Surgeon. This morning, as we were both in the great room (I mean a room which is eight or nine feet wide) I saw this surgeon looking into a quarto book, which I perceived to be an Italian dictionary. Do you read Italian, Sir? "I have been "studying it a while, Sir, but I cannot "say that I know much of it."

These were the first words I heard him utter, for he looks very reserv'd. Sir, said I, I know something of Italian myself; and if you chuse, we will read a page or two together out of any book you have. With all my heart, said he; and fetch'd a volume of Redi's medical consultations. I read a few periods, and as fluently as if it had been my own language. He was astonished at my readiness, as he had not yet found by my pronounciation that I was no Englishman. You read it, said he, much better than I. Were you ever in Italy? Ay, said I, I was only born and bred there, and was moreover the very

identical

identical compiler of this dictionary. The Scotchman (for he is a Scotchman) seem'd extremely pleased with this kind of adventure, and we are already very intimate friends. He speaks Spanish and Portuguese, besides some other languages; has been in all the four quarters of the world playing the surgeon on board this and that ship, and seems well skilled in his profession. Was it possible to form a better acquaintance in the midst of the Atlantic Ocean? He plays, besides, on the bag-pipe; an odd instrument I never saw in Italy. Our mountaneers indeed have the bag-pipe, but different from his. They introduce the air into the bag by blowing continually into a tube while they are playing: but he swells it by means of a bellows, which he presses with his left elbow, while he is managing the flute with his fingers. A very good contrivance to spare one's lungs! We are resolved to read a good deal of Italian and Portuguese before we reach Lisbon.

I aſk him numberleſs queſtions about Malabar and Madagaſcar, and tell him, by way of exchange, all that I know of Milan and Venice. Be no longer concerned at my ſituation: I am very well off; and this voyage ſhall be chearfully performed.

I promiſed yeſterday to ſpeak a little more of the Engliſh. Let us then begin with the Ladies, the beſt ſubject in the whole world to write upon.

And are the Engliſh Ladies handſomer than ours? Upon my word I expected this to be your firſt queſtion. But, firſt or laſt, the anſwer requires ſome conſideration: Nay, I will not anſwer it at all. I will only tell you a bit of converſation I had once with an able painter of ours, who has lived many years in England as well as myſelf. I aſk'd him once this ſame queſtion; and his anſwer was, that in Italy he has ſeen more Juno's than in England; but that in England there are more Venus's than in Italy.

How-

However you muſt not conclude from this, continued he, that the Italian beauties are all in the grand ſtile, and all the Engliſh in the lovely. There are many pretty women in Italy too, and many very majeſtic in England. But, in general, the Britiſh have more delicate complexions than ours, and ours more determinate features *(fattezze riſolute* was the phraſe) than theirs. Look at the ſkins and ſhapes at Ranelagh. Do you ever ſee any thing in Italy ſo bright and ſo tempting? But then look at the noſes of our Roman Ladies, look at the lips of the Neapolitan, look at the whole form of the Lombard and Venetian! Is there any thing properer for a Raphael to paint, or a Michelangelo to carve? In another thing, beſides, our Italians excel. No eyes in the world like thoſe of Italy for ſtriking you dead at once.

Hang your eyes and eye-brows, ſaid I peeviſhly. I care not a farthing for eyes or ſkins, for lips and chins, for noſes and ſhapes.

shapes. What's all this to me? I am intirely for sense, wit, and goodness, which are the true sources of amiableness in the fair. This is what we ought to mind, and not your fooleries about Juno's and Venus's. And will you say, that in point of wit, sense, and goodness, the Italian Ladies can vie with the English?

The painter seeing me grow so angry, ran away, crying that he would not listen any longer to a traytor to his country: thus I lost a fine opportunity of showing my skill in debating a question.

LETTER XII.

Tediousness. Vain efforts to drive it away.

King-George-Packet, Aug. 27, early in the morning.

IT was impossible yesterday to make use of my quill, because of a flat calm that made me sick. About sun-set a gale sprung up, and I could eat a bit of biscuit, drink a glass, and go to bed without being carried.

At

At five this morning I got up, not at all chearful. You never saw me in so brown a humour. I went upon deck, and sat there a full hour in perfect idleness. It is now past six, and I am still torpid, and my mind seems unwilling to be put in motion. Yet my mind is not a bottle of claret, that must be handled gently: so I will shake it, and force it to guide this quill until I am called to breakfast.

Vile dead weather that of yesterday! I know now what a calm is, and am sure storms are better by half. The captain says the contrary, but I will not believe a word about it. Did not the calm make me sick? Nor is it possible to describe the horror of that disorder called the sea-sickness! He must be an orator that can. You groan in spight of yourself: you growl like a wounded wolf, if wolves growl when they are wounded, which is a thing I am not sure of: you are ill, vastly ill, prodigiously ill! and yet, the

more

more sick you are, the more these seafaring folks go on repeating, that 'tis nothing, nothing indeed, nothing at all. Now heartily I could thrash them, if I durst, for terming nothing so dreadful a torment! and yet they must be right, for they must know better than I.

Nor is that hateful sickness the only plague one has on board a packet. There is another to be encounter'd, named Tediousness, which is full as great, full as detestable. And how can I help myself against it? I may stay below in my room, or I may stay upon deck. If I stay below, I cannot have any company, save that of my own self, which is pretty tolerable company as long as I can write. But can I write for ever? I grow presently tired of it; and tediousness lays hold of me if I do not run up-stairs. Well, I run up-stairs. But what can I do when I am there? I look at a very tall may-pole here, and at another there. They both support some pieces of canvass that hang

loose

loose in a calm, or catch the wind as it happens to stir. Do I look at any thing else? Yes: at two rows of brass-guns that never will let me hear their voices, on the frivolous pretence that no Monsieur will come near enough to be spoke to. What else can I cast my eyes upon? A boundless plain that struck me once with its immense expansion, rendered infinitely awful for a moment or two by an interminable uniformity, and irresistibly tremendous by its massy solemn undulation. The object is grand, prodigiously grand! But I have look'd at it so long, that familiarity has had its usual effect, and I cannot bear any longer that invariable expansion and invariable undulation. I find that nothing can please me long but what can talk; and the ocean cannot talk!

Here you will say, that a man used to think, might beguile one hour after another even in a dark dungeon, if he would but exert his mental powers and think away without intermission. How pretty

pretty this in speculation! But where is the man who can always call forth thoughts, and force them to dance in his presence as he pleases? Whatever you may do where you are, I cannot in this packet. I have often endeavoured to create an object; and, to tell you of one in particular, it is but a minute ago that I reached Turin, where you were impatiently waiting for my arrival. You all ran down stairs on hearing the rattle of my wheels and the claps of the postillion's whip. Six arms were extended to help me out of the chaise. One of you embraced me, one squeezed my hand, one was ready to cry for joy. Welcome, welcome, how do you do?

Had the illusion lasted, tediousness had kept at a distance. But my powers proved too weak, and it vanished away as soon as form'd. A beam crack'd, or a sailor swore, or a wave dash'd against the stern, and farewell illusion! There is no possibility on board a packet to build

build a caſtle in the air that is worth erecting! I put myſelf often in the poſture of Guido's famous Magdalen, my left elbow on my left knee, the knuckles of my left hand under my chin, and my eyes half ſhut. An excellent poſture for the purpoſe of building the ampleſt caſtle, with good ſolid walls, lofty turrets, and elevated battlements. But the fundamental brick is ſcarcely laid, that it is diſplaced by ſome unwelcome violence. When I was a boy it was one of my chief delights to ſtand watching a pretty circle which I had form'd on the ſmooth ſurface of a pond by throwing a ſmall pebble into it. But my ſchool-fellows, miſchief-making urchins, who preſently ſmoak'd me at my uſual diverſion, would pick up any thing that lay before them and fling it into the pond. My poor harmleſs circle was thus inceſſantly deſtroy'd by a thouſand others, broken, confuſed, and undiſtinguiſhable! Here is a ſimile for you! And have I not ſtolen

it

it from some English poet? I think I have; but cannot recollect from whom.

A fellow calls me to breakfast. When it is over I will beg a tune on the bag-pipe of my good surgeon: then we will read a while; and then come down to scribble again.

LETTER XIII.

A Bonito and the Flying-fish. Sea-voyages. Machinery in Epick Poems.

King-George-Packet, Aug. 27, aforenoon.

I Saw a thing just now that I had never seen before. A fish full five spans from head to tail. The sailors hook'd it in. They call it *Bonito*; a Spanish word that means *middling good*. I am to have my share of it at dinner by way of encouragement to eat, for the Captain swears I eat nothing: but this is to be understood only when I am sea-sick, as,

when

when I am well, I perform my duty as bravely as any man in the packet.

The hook with which the Bonito was caught, is near as big as my little finger, and the bait was a bit of rag wrapp'd round it, with the addition of two feathers clapp'd upon it in such a manner as aukwardly to resemble the *Flying-fish*, which Bonitos consider as a tit-bit. No creature but a silly fish could ever mistake a bit of rag for a dainty morsel.

The Flying-fish is about the size of a herring. Its fins are much larger in proportion than those of any other fish, and stand in the stead of wings. I have seen thousands of them to-day that darted out of the water, and flew, or rather flutter'd along in a straight line, the distance of two or three ships' length, then dropp'd down in their natural element.

I have never before seen a Flying-fish, nor a Bonito. So here are two new ideas fairly added to my stock. I am glad of

the

the addition though but small. Who knows but one day or other they may turn to good account? To point a moral, for instance, in speaking of some conqueror or some attorney? To bring about a new comparison between a poor hostess and some agent in Devonshire? We have never knowledge enough: we must always endeavour to heap up as much of it as we can. Every thing has its use upon occasion, and the poorest trifle will unexpectedly be of service in speech or in writing, in prose or in poetry.

The Bonito will come upon table within an hour: but I would rather it was an anchiovy, and be with you to eat it. I should like it better than the biggest inhabitant of the ocean in this packet. An irksome thing it is to go by sea! And yet I ought to be ashamed to say so, considering what a short voyage I am going. Lisbon must be looked upon as next door to Falmouth when we think of the voyages of some Englishmen, Dutchmen, French-

Frenchmen, Spaniards, and other people. But I am a traveller like Ulysses, who went a while up and down the Mediterranean, and made as great a pother about it as if he had gone from Ithaca to Japan by Terra del Fuego, and back again another way. Fifty thousand people, nay, fifty hundred thousand, who were neither kings nor heroes, have gone twenty times as far, and no Mæonian bard dreamed of composing epic poems upon any of them. The only epic poem that ever was written since that of Homer to celebrate a man who had gone a long voyage, was the performance of a Spaniard. I must tell you the story to lengthen my letter.

This Spaniard (Erçilla was his name) perfectly aware that no modern bard would ever trouble his head about any man who went a few thousand miles by water, having been so far as Peru, (if I mistake not) resolved to be himself his own Homer.

In consequence of this resolution, he sat down to his desk; and after having invoked Apollo and the Muses, rhymed a long epic poem, of which his voyage was the subject, and himself the principal Hero.

After this example I have a mind to write the *Olisipossey,* or an epic account of my voyage from Falmouth to (*a*) Olisipo, alias Lisbon. As for a hero, I am not at all afraid of wanting one of the very first magnitude; and as for subaltern characters my good surgeon is ready at hand for an Achilles, Mr. Bawn for a Hector, and Mr. Oak for a Diomedes, an Ajax, a Nestor, or any thing. The cabbin-boy himself might be made good use of for a Patroclus, an Automedon, or a Calchas.

But without machinery an epic poem is not worth a farthing; and how shall I con-

---

(*a*) *That Lisbon was once called* OLISIPO *appears from a ancient inscription. It was also called* ULYSIBONA, ULYSIPONA, *and* FELICITAS JULIA.

I contrive it? In times of yore machinery was always ready. Jupiter, Juno, Venus, Minerva, Neptune, Mars, and other celestials were kind enough to fly to the assistance of a distressed poet. Strange beings besides, that were half girls and half fish, were to be met almost on any voyage, and they would sing airs and duos by the side of the ship, and play a thousand gambols on the water. Ulysses himself met with some of them in the gulf of Naples, and an Archbishop, who was a kind of Greek poet in French prose, has informed us that Telemachus, the eldest son of Ulysses, met once a very fine lady sitting in state on an enormous shell of an oyster, and rambling at a great distance from the shore round the island of Cyprus or Crete (I forget which) with a whole orchestra of fiddlers and pipers, some swimming along by the help of their tails, some sitting upon dolphins and sharks, and some riding upon crabs and lobsters.

This indeed was fine machinery. But, alas, it is all forestalled! and should I make use of it, there is no puny Critic amongst the puny Reviewers of England, but what would call me a plagiary!

The good times for machinery are over, and now instead of Syrens and Tritons we meet in our voyages with nothing else but a Bonito and a Flying-fish; and surely neither the Flying-fish nor the Bonito can be made use of in this critical age by way of machinery.

I must therefore drop the scheme of the *Olisipossey*, as I have not invention enough to overcome this difficulty: and instead of lamenting that neither Syren nor Triton will come to sing *Care luci*, or pipe upon their shells about this packet, I must endeavour to be pleased when my honest Scotchman presses the bellows of his bag-pipe with his elbow.

LETTER XIV.

Life led in a Packet. The beneficial effects of a dinner. Several thousand reis are no riches.

King-George-Packet, Aug. 27. towards evening.

I Ought not to mention the Bonito again. You must have had enough of it. Yet the conveniency of beginning a new letter without taking the trouble of thinking about a pretty exordium, makes me tell you, that Bonito is a very improper name for such a fish; because, instead of being but *middling good*, it is in fact *exceedingly good*.

But what shall I say next? I will acquaint you with the tenour of life in this packet.

You know already that in the morning I get up, sometimes sooner sometimes later. You know likewise that when I am up, either I do something, or I do nothing; read, or read not; write, or write not: and you can guess that about eight

I breakfaſt *Anglicè* upon tea and toaſt, or bread and butter: this cuſtom however I intend to break myſelf of; and as ſoon as I am in Portugal I propoſe to reaſſume that of falling early upon grapes, figs, and melons, in order to qualify myſelf again for my native country, that I may not be a foreigner at home.

The time between breakfaſt and dinner I fill up as well as I can. My book and my quill, *cela va sans dire*. Sometimes I walk; and the deck is long enough for it, as it is exactly thirty three of my ſteps and a ſhoe over. Yet this exerciſe proves often inconvenient, as I am not uſed to move like a crab, leaning on one ſide, in order to adapt my body to the inclination of the packet, which hangs often on the larboard or the ſtarboard ſide, according as the wind blows. Therefore, when I cannot walk, or am tired of it as well as of reading and writing, I ſit idle.

As for confabulation I have not much of it. The ſurgeon is far from being talkative.

talkative. The Captain and Mr. Oak mind the altitude and the latitude; so that, when we have got some intelligence about each other's health in the morning, praised the weather at noon, and heard how many knots we go towards evening, there is almost an end of our converse.

But dinner comes upon table. And here let me tell you that I need none of your pity, as our dinner is always so ample that it would suffice a dozen friars after the most rigid fast.

This indeed is the very best hour of all the four and twenty, and the only one that deserves to be painted with pretty butter-fly wings like the handsomest of those three which have been introduced by Raphael in his wedding of Cupid and Psyche, perhaps to give a hint that a wedding-dinner ought to last three hours.

But do you get new bread every day?

Yes: here is a baker on board, Madam, that makes it.

But your meat is falted?

Not at all, Madam, excepting the beef. The mutton is frefh, becaufe we have live fheep on board. We have alfo a pretty grunting pig, and fo many cages full of poultry, as would laft us two months and more, if we were to be two months at fea.

No child in England would want fuch details; but our land-lock'd Ladies on the other fide the Alps muft be told the minuteft particulars; and I will always fubmit to any drudgery to give their curiofity moft ample fatisfaction.

By this account you fee how well we employ the dining hour. With that hour fome fpeculatifts have found great fault, and bitterly bemoaned the neceffity men are under of eating their dinners. If men, faid one of them, were freed from that neceffity, and of courfe not obliged to contrive how to provide themfelves with victuals, which takes up almoft all their time, they would undeniably have more leifure leisure for the cultivation of their understandings; for attending to sciences and arts, to manufactures and commerce.

But, gentlemen, if I may dare to speak my mind amongst you, let me say that just the contrary would happen. If we were not forced to think after the means of filling our bellies, would we not one and all sink into idleness? Why do the learned make books, lawyers defend property, physicians feel the pulse, astronomers gaze at the zodiack, husbandmen plow, masons build, tailors sew, and soldiers fight, but for the sake of procuring a dinner? Strike off this necessity, and there is an end of every thing good, desirable, and laudable. The more I think on it, the more I say with the Bergamasco (you remember that ballad-singer) whose song always ended with the burthen:

> *Tuto tuto in questo mondo*
> *Che se fa de bel e de bon,*
> *L' è per un piato de Maccaron.*

However, be this as it will, our dinner here is seldom protracted beyond an hour. The Captain, Mr. Oak, the Surgeon, and myself are sober men, and commonly make an end of it as soon as the second bottle is over. Then I walk, or sit, or read, or write, or listen to the bag-pipe, until the sun goes down and leaves me at liberty to look a while at the greater or lesser bear. Towards nine I call for a bisket and a glass of Madeira, and then go to bed.

This is the story *à peu prés* of every day; nor can any of you, as I conceive, find the least fault with such a regular and innocent manner of spending time.

But you go to bed, you say: and pray, what sort of bed have you got?

My bed is a thing placed in a dark closet, and clapp'd betwixt two planks, as one may say: so that it looks something like a trunk without a lid. *Couch* might possibly be a fitter name for it than *Bed*.

But

But here I would not have you think that I have my meat and drink with this bed, merely becauſe I have a plain unmeaning face. You would be miſtaken if you ſhould ſuppoſe it. Beſides the four guineas I paid the king at Falmouth for the permiſſion to embark in a packet of his, on my arrival in *Portingal* (as the ſailors ſay) I am to pay the Captain twenty three thouſand reis.

What a frightful ſum! And how rich muſt he be who can pay off ſo many thouſand!

Do not let imagination carry you too far. Twenty three thouſand reis make no more than five moidores: ſo that, if the voyage and my preſent appetite laſt long, Captain Bawn will be half undone. Beſides that to make ſure of a ſhort voyage I would willingly ſubmit to pay him ſome thouſand reis more. Be it ſhort or long, it is quite plain that I muſt be a gainer by the bargain.

LET-

LETTER XV.

Beauty of a Night at Sea. Three Ships pursuing.

King-George Packet, Aug. 28, 1760.

LAST night the motion of the packet was very violent and very disagreeable. But so much the better, because we also went at a greater rate than usual.

Finding it impossible to sleep in that motion, I crawled off my couch a little after midnight and went upon deck, where I employ'd both my eyes in looking at the packet, at the foaming billows, at both the bears, and at the other heavenly lights over-head.

All these objects put together form a spectacle by moon-light which is really glorious. The packet itself (which is certainly less than nothing when the eye of the mind compares it with the ocean and the heavens) the packet, I say, in the bodily

bodily eye of such a poor narrow-minded mortal as I am, makes a magnificent figure on the waves, adds much to that glorious spectacle, and challenges a very considerable share of admiration.

It was between two and three this morning when a little roguish fellow who stood on the mast-head, descried three sails which he took to be in full chace of us.

As the uniform tenour of my present life leaves me a constant prey to tediousness, I think I felt some little tickling pleasure on the sudden hearing of the usual cry *a sail, a sail*: and I am really of opinion that in my irksome situation it would not displease me much to have a dozen bullets interchanged with an enemy in what they call a running fight.

Mr. Oak was then upon deck, and the Captain was soon call'd; nor did the Surgeon stay long before he came too. It was not long before we all could distinctly see three clouds of canvas that
were

were driven towards us. The Captain foon concluded they were three men of war, and fwore that they were Englifh. However, not chufing to venture a parley for fear of miftake, we crouded inftantly as much fail as the packet could bear, and flipp'd away in fpight of all the efforts we fuppofed they made to overtake us. The chace lafted full four hours, and when Mr. Oak faw them give up the point, was quite pofitive they had known us by the fwiftnefs of our failing, and that they are a part of Commodore Edgecombe's fquadron.

This little adventure, and fome diftant poffibility of a pretty combat, raifed my fpirits fo well, that I chofe to ftay upon deck till dinner, which was not performed in filence, as we had all fomething to fay about the three fails; a fubject that was not exhaufted till we could talk of *Cape Finifterre*, of which about four in the afternoon we had a confufed fight.

I was

I was much comforted to hear that if the wind holds but two days longer, we shall be at Lisbon on Sunday, as it is but three hundred miles off. This is good news, considering how tired I am with my voyage, though it has to this hour been as prosperous as we could wish, excepting the calm on the second day.

LETTER XVI.

A hole in the Cabbin why and what for.

King-George-Packet, Aug. 29, 1760.

IN the midst of the great cabbin I took notice to day of a square bit of a plank, which is moveable. I asked the Surgeon about it, and this is the substance of the information that I got with regard to a hole which is covered by that moveable plank.

Almost every week a packet sails from Falmouth to Lisbon with only the mail that is sent from London. Mails are not heavy cargoes: but when a packet sails back to England, besides the returning mail, it has that hole fill'd with so many bags of Portugal-coin, as often amount from thirty to fifty, and even sixty thousand pounds sterling. A round sum when we look into the almanack, and find that every year has two and fifty weeks.

Those bags are deliver'd to the Captains of the packets by the English merchants at Lisbon, and put by the Captain into the hole in the great cabbin; and it has happen'd some weeks, that the bags proved so numerous as partly to obstruct the usual celerity of their sailing. And this was the case once, that a packet called the *Prince Frederic* was actually taken by a Barbary Pirate with no less than eighty thousand pounds sterling in the hole.

You may now guess why we are not afraid of pursuers. No vessel is turned into a packet but what is a prime sailer, and all possible care is also taken both at Falmouth and Lisbon to clean them so well

well before they put to sea, that they swim along like dolphins.

I need not tell you that the Portuguese (considering King and people together) are very rich in gold and jewels. Their riches however are not the product of Portugal, but of their ultramarine settlements: and I have often heard it affirm'd with confidence, that from Brasil alone they draw yearly above two millions sterling. As to Portugal itself, its products are but scanty and its manufactures inconsiderable. The only things that it yields in very great plenty, are oranges, lemons, and wine. Of these the English buy up large quantities; but still the balance of trade rises high in their favour, as the Portuguese get from them many articles both for home and for their settlements abroad. Therefore the surplus due to England is paid by Portugal in gold; and this gold goes every week into the holes in the cabin.

See how the things of this world are equipoifed! The Portuguefe want the conveniencies which the Englifh have the induftry to make, and the Englifh want the gold which the Portuguefe draw from the Brafils; and thus both nations do each other's bufinefs.

The French and the Dutch have long fought to gain from the Englifh a commerce fo beneficial. But I have a notion their fchemes will hardly ever take, for two reafons. The one is, that the Englifh are much ftronger at fea than both the French and Dutch together: and there is fomething in fuperior ftrength, that will carry any point amongft nations as well as amongft individuals. The other reafon is, that neither the Dutch nor the French could buy from the Portuguefe thofe large quantities of fruit and wine which the Englifh take in part of payment for what they furnifh. Suppofe even the Portugefe fhould be willing to have the greateft part of what they want

want either from the French or the Dutch rather than from the English, the English would presently make them change their mind, even without going to war for it. They have but to provide themselves with wine and fruit from some other country, and the Portuguese are half undone.

It is therefore most probable, that the commerce of Portugal will not be lost to England as long as its inhabitants are fond of the bowl and the bottle, even on the supposition that the French naval force should increase and the English decrease, which, as far as human foresight can go, will not be the case tomorrow. The English are in a fair way to come off quite victorious this war: and if they do, what power for centuries to come will dare to control their will on the ocean, and what ship sail to Portugal or any where else but by their permission?

LETTER XVII.

Vain wishes or castle-building. Study hard. Pronounciation how attained. The Rock, the Rock.

King-George-Packet, Aug. 30, 1760.

LISTEN with attention to every thing you hear in the short space of a day, and I am widely mistaken if you do not find that there is no man living but who wishes every day of his life for something quite impossible for him ever to obtain.

Every man living is thoroughly persuaded that vain wishes are no less ridiculous than absurd; and yet do but stretch your hand, and you will certainly touch a mortal who secretly wishes to be possess'd of such opulence as Cresus never had, of such power as Kulikan had been ashamed to claim, or of such beauty as Circassia could never produce.

I will

I will not set about to enquire whether this universal proneness to wish for impossibilities is a lamentable depravation of our minds, or a quality designedly given us by nature for very good purposes. Be this as it will, I will take the liberty to advise my friends never to suffer long such extravagant wanderings of their imaginations: for, besides that the character of an ethereal brick-layer is absurd and ridiculous, a man who does not get the habit of checking his thoughts when they run wild about, will insensibly lose much of that activity which his circumstances in life may possibly require. By mere wishing nothing is gotten: but by a vigorous and unremitted use even of indifferent abilities, it is very near certain that many things may be obtained very well worth a man's wishing.

I was led into this train of thinking by overhearing one of the sailors wish just now, that he could speak the language in which I was addressing my good surgeon.

surgeon. This put me in mind of Sir Arthur and Sir Marmaduke, two worthy knights of my acquaintance, one of whom wish'd often in my hearing that he knew Latin, and the other Greek. But dear knights, said I to them, instead of repeating your wishes for these ten years past, as you have done, why did you not lay violent hands upon the Port-Royal-Grammars, or any book that might have been conducive to that end which you seem to think would have made you both prodigiously happy?

A language is not like the heart of a maiden, of which the possession sometimes depends on us, and sometimes not. A man really desirous to know a language, be it Latin or Greek, Arabic or Ethiopic, will certainly make himself master of it, if he will but sit down and do what I am actually doing.

And what are you actually doing?

I am studying Portuguese like a dragon, and am about it three or four hours every day.

day. A fortnight or three weeks before I left London I did very near the same; and all along the road from Plymouth to Falmouth never did I cease in my chaise to peep into a Portuguese book: so that, if I do not understand the very pilot who shall steer us up the Tagus to Lisbon, I will think myself such a knight as Sir Arthur or Sir Marmaduke.

But, brothers, I see you laugh. What do you laugh at?

We laugh at your boast, Sir.

Tout doucement, Mesdames, as people will often say in France. To learn a language in a month I think impossible as well as you. But as to the enabling myself to understand the pilot in a month, you will recollect that I have known the Spanish tongue these five and twenty years, and that the Portuguese is but a dialect of the Spanish; nor do I think that it differs quite so much from it as the dialect of Venice does from the language of Tuscany. Then, I intend not to be a critic in the Lufitanic and mafter all its niceties and prettineſſes. I want no more of it than will decently help me on while I ſtay in Portugal: and ſo you fee that my confidence as to the pilot, is not quite ſo ill-grounded as you thought.

I will not let this opportunity ſlip of telling you, that there is an infallible way to give your little ſon a facility of pronouncing any language, if you intend to make him learn more than one. Lend me your ear, and I will tell you how this may be done.

Our people of rank at Turin have got a notion, that their children muſt never be ſuffered to ſpeak any Piedmonteſe but what is ſpoken in the metropolis; and in conſequence of this notion they keep a ſtrict watch upon the poor little things for fear they ſhould catch the clowniſh accent on the oppoſite ſide of the Po.

This practice is wrong, and I wiſh you may never adopt it. Let the boy learn the

the polite fpeech of his town; but be not afraid to let him learn likewife that of the peafants : nay, encourage him to mimick their talk. By making him learn two fpeeches inftead of one, you will enable him to articulate more founds than by his learning only one. And if it is in your power, I would even have you fhift him from place to place while his organs of fpeech are yet tender and pliant, and bring him to mimick any uncouth fpeech of Piedmont or Monferrat. Take him likewife frequently to the play, and make him mind the different Italian dialects fpoken by the Dramatis Perfonæ, and repeat as much of their nonfenfe as it is poffible. Nothing will ever fpoil his polite Piedmontefe when he hears it conftantly fpoke at home; and yet numberlefs are the founds that he will certainly enable himfelf to form, if you will but put him thus in the way.

Many Italians are to be found in Paris and in London, who in a very little time

fpeak

speak French and English with such a right pronounciation as to be mistaken for natives. The reason is, that Italy abounds more with different dialects than any other country of the same dimension, and that few are its inhabitants but what know more than one, either by moving from place to place, or by going to those plays in which every interlocutor speaks the dialect of his own town.

On the other hand you do not meet with a French gentleman in a hundred able to pronounce a foreign language right, not even when he has studied it a great while, and when he can speak it with purity of phraseology and grammatical correctness. No other reason can be assigned for this, but that in his infancy his Mamma was terrified when she caught him in the abominable act of uttering any sound that border'd on the *poissard* or the *badaut*, and reprimanded him with such severity as if he had committed a great crime. He was thus
brought

brought up with an untractable tongue that never will utter any sound but what is genuine Gallic.

But, Sir, come upon deck, and you will see the Rock. The Rock I suspect to be some part of the Portugal coast; and so farewel in haste.

LETTER XVIII.

Navigation ended. Batiste and Kelly. Plunge or pay. Banks of the Tagus.

Lisbon, Aug. 30, 1760. about midnight.

LOOK at the date, and give me joy. We landed this evening about eight o'clock. I was very glad to be rid of my floating habitation; yet sorry to leave the Captain, the Lieutenant, and my good Surgeon. They have treated me with kindness and civility, for which I shall remember them as long as I live.

Well; I am landed: and there is an end of navigation. But I thought it very odd that when first on shore I could not

stand

stand upon my legs, but tottered to the right and the left, as if my blood had been in an undulating motion. This difficulty of standing and walking with a steady foot was not the effect of any giddiness. I cannot tell what it was, but it seem'd as if the ground had moved like a ship: yet in the ship I could stand or walk very well, and, as I thought, without tottering. Thus unable when I landed to make use of my legs, I was obliged to hire a man who handed me for about a mile to a coffee-house. The odd motion of my blood subsided by degrees as I went on, and in less than two hours I was again like myself.

From the coffee-house I sent my helper to enquire after one *Batiste*, a faithful French servant I had formerly in London. He was presently found out; and hearing of my unexpected arrival, rose hastily from supper and came to me quite out of breath with running, his countenance full of joy and surprise.

This

This *Batiste* took me to one *Kelly*, an old Irishman who keeps a kind of an inn on the summit of a hill called *Buenos Aires*. I was quite fatigued when we reach'd it. Here I have taken up my quarters for the time I shall stay in Lisbon; and now let me come to the conclusion of my voyage.

It was about ten in the morning when our people had a full view of the *Rock of Lisbon*; that is, of a very high promontory on the left hand as you enter the Tagus, and at no great distance from the mouth of it.

That promontory looks perfectly barren, and has the appearance of a huge heap of rugged stones. Yet I am told that up and down it, there are many fine spots; that in the lower parts it is embellished with vineyards; that in several places it is covered with trees; and that it has even some flats where sheep and cattle are grazing.

I am

I am told further that on the utmost top of it, there is a convent cut into the rock itself, called the *Cork-convent* by the sailors, because the friars there have most of their utensils and furniture made of cork, as the place is so damp, that they cannot have them of any other material. In short so many curious things were told me about that rock and about the situation and form of that convent, that I have some desire to go and see it. But we will think of this another time. Let us for the present go on with the interesting story of this day.

When the Rock was full in view I was called upon deck. There a sailor stood up to me, and informed me with a civil saucy face, that it was the sailors' custom to duck in the sea any body who saw the Rock for the first time; and as that happened to be my case, he humbly desired my compliance with that custom by stripping immediately, except I rather chose

chose to be duck'd with my cloaths on my back.

This unexpected address did not startle me much, as it occur'd directly, that this was nothing more than a harmless scheme to get a little drink-money. However, to encrease the humour of it I made myself as serious as an old bear, and speaking slow and loud that I might be heard from deck to deck, " Sir, said
" I, you and your companions are wel-
" come to drown me, if you think it
" proper; you know, Sir, that I cannot
" be so ridiculous as to attempt the least
" resistance against a body of men who
" would drown an army of Frenchmen,
" if justly provoked. As to the ceremony,
" I certainly should have no objection,
" were the ocean an ocean of Dorchester-
" beer or London-porter: yet, as it hap-
" pens that it is made of a liquor I always
" had an unconquerable abhorrence of,
" I would rather compound the matter;
" and if any body else, you yourself for
" instance,

"inſtance, ſhould be ſo generous as to be duck'd or drown'd in my ſtead, I would endeavour to convince you and this honorable company that my predominant vice is not ingratitude."

"Sir," replied Jack, "give me your hand for that, you are a Gentleman; and, Sir, if I can be of ſervice (and here he ſwore a pretty oath) you are welcome; and I don't care (another oath) if I am ever ſo well duck'd for the ſake of a Gentleman."

To make ſhort, he ſtripp'd to the trowſers in an inſtant. His companions put him in a wooden frame that went round his breaſt under the arm-pits. The frame was tied to a pulley; the pulley faſtened to the extremity of a beam which lay acroſs the maſt-head; ſome of them drew him up, then let go the rope; and plump went the raſcal into the middle of a wave from a height of at leaſt five and twenty feet. The plunge was repeated ſeveral times

times in spight of his cries, to the no small diversion of the company.

The fellow being taken out of the frame, came up to me again, and wet as he was wanted to clasp me into his arms as a brother-sailor now that I had duely seen the Rock; but a piece of money rescued me from his embraces.

As we approached the mouth of the Tagus a signal was made to a fisherman to come to us and be our pilot: not that we stood in need of any, as our people knew the river quite as well as any Portuguese. But the Captains of packets must comply with their instructions, by which they are order'd not to enter the Tagus without a Portuguese pilot. The fellow we got is a mulatto so very like a monkey, that his dirty hat and tatter'd cloaths could hardly make me think him a human being. He came to us directly and leapt on board from his boat; and as we went over the bar, to shew his skill in conducting ships, he made a thoufand ſtrange faces and contorſions, beckoning (with his lips pouting inſtead of uſing words) to ſome of our ſailors in his boat, to row this way and that way, that we might follow with ſafety.

Going thus up the river I viewed the ſhore on the left hand of us. There are ſeveral fortifications from place to place, beſides numberleſs buildings. We ſtopp'd a moment oppoſite a tower built in the river, to hear what a fellow there had to ſay to us through a ſpeaking trumpet. That tower is fortified, and looks handſome at ſome diſtance. Having anſwer'd with a loud voice ſome few queſtions aſk'd from thence, and told what the ſhip was, we continued our way up, and preſently ſaw the royal village of Bellem, where I am told that the King has reſided ever ſince the earthquake.

In the neighbourhood of a town lately deſtroy'd, I did not think I ſhould ſee ſuch a vaſt number of edifices as there are: but the Surgeon told me that the earthquake

quake vented itself chiefly upon Lisbon, and caused little damage from Bellem down to the sea. It would have been a vast addition to the calamity Lisbon has suffer'd had so many buildings been destroy'd, to the utter ruin of the many thousands who live along that shore. Those buildings, some of which appear to be of a noble construction, are all white on the outside, with lattices and window-shutters painted green, which have a fine effect from the river. Many of the houses have gardens and terrasses ornamented with vases, statues, turrets, and obelisks; and withal so many trees round them, that the *coup d' oeuil* is render'd one of the grandest and most picturesque. Nothing can equal it that ever I saw, except Genoa with its suburbs.

I imagine that all this proves much less striking when view'd near and walking along-shore, because the sight cannot embrace so many objects at once, as it does from a distance, nor discriminate the ugly parts: But the whole surveyed from the middle of the river looks like the work of some benevolent Necromancer.

The Tagus is about two miles broad at the mouth; but widens by degrees as you go up, and overagainst the town is nine or ten miles broad. Lisbon is about fifteen miles distant from the mouth: but as it was quite dark when I reach'd it, I did not see it. To-morrow my excursions will begin, and, I hope, furnish matter for several letters.

Let me now cast my eyes round my new dwelling. I have four little rooms in a line on the ground floor; that is, almost the whole house, which is one of the many that have been built since the earthquake. For himself, wife, and children, my landlord Kelly has but two small rooms and a kitchen left. From one window he tells me that to-morrow I shall see the river full of ships, and have other fine prospects from the other windows.

LETTER XIX.

Pretty Polly's marriage. Bull-fight at Campo Pequeno. Lusitanian Pick-pockets. Dwarfish men and women.

Lisbon, Aug. 31, 1760.

TO day was Sunday: and how do you think I have spent the afternoon? I will tell you by and by. Let me first say something of the morning.

I got up about nine; and while I was busying myself about some luscious grapes, behold *Batiste* alighting from a fine Spanish horse, and a moment after *his wife* from a chaise drawn by two mules, and led by as fine a blackamoor as king Jarba in *Metastasio*'s Dido. Ah! How do you do, my little *Polly?* And abruptly kiss'd her in the face of the sun, perfectly forgetting that I was in Portugal where women must not be kiss'd in the face of the sun. But one is so glad to see old friends!

It was in London where I firſt knew this Polly, a pretty and modeſt girl. Batiſte left my ſervice to follow her to Portugal, where ſhe went to live with an old aunt who was to bequeath her all ſhe had, and that *all* was no inconſiderable a fortune for a girl who had nothing but a pretty face and no inclination to hire it. The fellow was madly in love with her, and ſhe had no averſion to him; but the aunt was ſomewhat croſs, and would not have her marry juſt turned of fifteen. The earthquake render'd him her huſband ſooner than he expected, and in a manner ſo peculiarly uncommon, that I cannot forbear to relate it: nor do you tell me that it looks odd for a maſter to be the Hiſtorian of his ſervant, becauſe a good ſervant in my opinion is a hero, and full as valuable as any other human being.

Batiſte had juſt walked out of the town on the morning when the earthquake happened. Seeing the houſes tumble on all

all sides, instead of stopping where he was, as some other *Innamorato* would probably have done, he ran precipitously back to the town and towards the house where his mistress liv'd, and had the incredible good luck of spying her on a heap of ruins where she had fallen in a fit while she was endeavoring her escape. Had he tarried but a few moments longer, she would have perished in the flames that broke out around her in a hundred places. Without staying to examine whether she were dead or alive, he threw her over his shoulders, and fortune befriended him so compleatly that he carried his burthen safe out of the town, though many buildings continued to fall about his ears, and though fire surrounded him on all sides.

The poor thing came to herself as they came out of the danger. They both look'd at the immense desolation that was left behind, both scream'd, and wept, and did not know what to do. The houses

houses still tumbled and the fire still broke out in every part, which made them think that the poor aunt was buried in the ruins. They grew impatient to be far from such immense misery, and immediately resolv'd to go back to England. Both had some little money about them; therefore, not well knowing what they were doing, they took the road to Spain. At *Badajoz*, *Madrid*, and other places they met with some charitable relief; but no great matter, it seems, for fifteen months after the earthquake they reached London in a most miserable plight.

When they came to me there, Polly had a girl in her arms about three months old; but they had married in France a little before the birth of the child, as I was convinced by their certificates. Polly, Polly, (said I, after having read them) and so you are married? What could I do? (answer'd she, blushing up to her eyes). Sir, we were alone, and he swore so much he would always be true! Here she cried and kiss'd her child; and I kiss'd her that she might not think me too severe a censurer.

I thought it a dream when they first made their appearance, as the old aunt had long before written word from Lisbon to some relation, that they had both perished in the earthquake. I told them this, and they apprised her by letter of the contrary. The poor old woman was transported with joy and thankfulness at the unexpected news, and insisted upon their going back to her, acquainting them that she had been lucky enough to save something out of her former fortune, and they complied with her desire. But she did not enjoy them long, for she died soon after their arrival, leaving them about a hundred moidores, which was all that she had. With this little stock Batiste turn'd out a Jack of all trades and Polly took kindly to her needle. Thus I found them every day

more

more happy in each other and in their little girl; and as they are both induſtrious and laborious, I do not doubt but their circumſtances will grow better and better.

Now, ſaid I, what is the meaning of that chaiſe and that horſe?

Sir, ſaid Batiſte, they are for you. You cannot go afoot about this town, except you chuſe to be melted by the heat or kill'd by the fatigue of going up-hill and down-hill. You muſt have a chaiſe during the time you ſtay here, and I am to attend you on horſeback.

Well, ſaid I: you muſt know better what I am to do in Liſbon; and ſo we will have the chaiſe and the horſe.

After dinner I got into the chaiſe attended as above, and the Negro trotted to a place called *Campo Pequeno*, which is about four miles (perhaps five or ſix) from the town, where I was to ſee what they call the bull-feaſt or bull-hunting. But before I attempt to deſcribe it, I

muſt

must premise that being just come from a country where the Lord's day is not openly prophaned, I could not help being shock'd to see so many Christians, and especially so many Priests and Friars, present at such a diversion, which to me seem'd the most inhuman that ever could be invented by men, next the combats of the gladiators in ancient Rome.

At *Campo Pequeno* a wooden edifice has been erected for the only purpose of exhibiting these barbarous entertainments. The edifice is an octagonal amphitheatre consisting of two rows of boxes, one row over the other, and the diameter of its area is, as I take it, about two hundred common steps.

None of the boxes has the least decoration, except those of the royal family which are hung with silken stuff. The row above is for the better sort, and that of the ground-floor for the populace, who are likewise admitted into the area, though their danger is not small of being

gored

gored or trampled by the bulls, whose marches and evolutions I take to be quite as rapid as those of the Prussian troops.

In the box where I took my seat there were but three people besides myself, though the box could contain ten or twelve. Two of the three had the appearance of gentlemen; the other was a Dominican Friar as lean as a lizzard.

Before the entertainment began I attempted some converse with them; but even the humble *Religiozo* seem'd to look upon me with disdain and contempt. They all answer'd my first words with so churlish an air, that I gave over presently, and like them kept silent the whole time.

How I came to disgust them thus at once, I cannot guess: but by their frequent and affected glances upon my coat, which I held up at last to the Friar, not without some resentment, that he might inspect it nearer, I suspected that they conceived a very low opinion of me for not being dress'd in silk like other gentlemen,

men. Yet it was not my fault, having not yet had time to do what I muſt do in this hot weather.

The King, whoſe box was not far from that in which I ſat, was dreſs'd in a plain ſky-blue with ſome diamonds about him. He had with him his own brother the Infant Don Pedro, who has lately married the King's eldeſt daughter call'd the Princeſs of Braſil.

The Queen was in another box with that Princeſs and her three other daughters all ſparkling with jewels.

In the area and juſt under the Queen's box there was a man on horſeback; a kind of herald, I thought; dreſs'd ſomewhat like one of our Neapolitan *Coviello's* in our plays, who held a long rod in his hand.

As the King came in, two triumphal cars very meanly adorned entered the area, each drawn by ſix mules. Eight black Africans were upon one, and eight copper-coloured Indians upon the other.

They

They made several caracols round; then all leapt from the cars and bravely fought an obstinate battle with wooden swords one band against the other. The Indians were soon slain by the Africans, and lay extended a while on the ground, shaking their legs in the air as if in the last convulsions, and rolling in the dust before they were quite dead. Then, like Bays's troops in the Rehearsal, both the dead and the living went to mix with the croud, while the cars drove away amidst the acclamations of the multitude, and made room for the two knights that were to fight the bulls.

These knights came in, both on horseback, dress'd after the ancient Spanish manner, made fine with many ribbonds of various colours, with feathers on their hats, each brandishing a long and thin spear. Their horses were beautiful, mettlesome, and gallantly accoutred. One of the hero's was clad in crimson, the other in yellow. Both look'd very

brisk,

brisk, and both paid their obeisance to the King, Queen, and people, making their horses kneel three times: then, clapping spurs, made them caper and vault a while round the area with a surprising dexterity.

When all this was over, the yellow champion placed himself over against the gate at which the bulls were to come out, and the crimson stood at some distance from him in the same direction. A man from without open'd the gate, and cover'd himself with it by getting behind. The bull bursts out and makes to the yellow knight who stands ready to receive him with his spear lifted high. The bull's horns had wooden knobs on their tips, that they might not gore the horse if they should reach him. The courageous yellow-knight push'd his spear at the beast, left half of it in his neck, and made his horse start aside in a moment. The wounded bull ran bellowing after him; but the knight wheeling round and

and round ſtuck two or three more ſpears into his neck and ſhoulders. The bull's rage, as you may imagine, encreaſed to a degree that impreſſed horrour: and now the crimſon-knight had his turn; for the beaſt made at him, but got nothing by changing his attack, except ſome more ſpears into ſeveral parts of his body, ſo that his blood ſpouted out in ſeveral rills.

When the bull began to remit his fury by loſs of blood, one of the champions drew a heavy broad-ſword, and gave him ſuch a cut on the back between the ribs, as almoſt cleft him to the middle. Down the poor beaſt fell with ſuch roaring as I think was heard at Liſbon. Then the man in the *Coviello*'s dreſs, ſeeing the final blow, gallopped ſtraight to the gate at which the triumphal cars had entered, and order'd in four mules which dragg'd the dying beaſt out of the amphitheatre, together with ſome of the populace who had got aſtride upon the bloody and mangled

mangled carcafe. The applaufe of the fpectators was very clamorous.

But I muft not omit to fay, that the two knights were not the only enemies the poor bull had to encounter. There were two other *Cavalleiro's* on foot, holding faft the tails of the two horfes, running as they ran, or ftopping as they ftopp'd, each fhaking a red filken cloak to frighten or rather exafperate the bull, while fome others, on foot likewife, flily wounded him with daggers in the fide and buttocks.

The agility of thefe foot-champions is beyond all belief. When the furious beaft made at any of them, they hopp'd afide and were out of danger. One of them feizing one of the bull's horns, fuffer'd himfelf to be dragg'd a while before he would let go his hold; gave him feveral cuts with a knife while he was thus dragg'd; then let himfelf fall, got on his legs in an inftant, and efcaped. But a little negro did ftill a bolder thing.

He stood full in the bull's way while running with the utmost fury, and just as I thought he was going to be lifted on his horns, took a spring on the bull's back and jump'd clean over him.

Eighteen were the bulls slaughter'd in this feast or hunting, and each with some variety of wanton cruelty. Spears were stuck into some of them that carried squibs and crackers, whose fire and noise was more troublesome than the wound. One of the most fierce leapt over the barrier of a box just under mine, and I expected him to do some mischief; but the Portuguese are well aware of such accidents, and the people in that box were quick to quit their seats, some throwing themselves over the barrier into the area, and some over the partitions into the next boxes. The bull embarrassed in the benches was presently dispatched by many swords.

The last bull however was very near revenging all the rest upon the crimson-knight

knight and his horſe. He ran them both down with a terrible ſhock; and had it not been for the knobs on his horns, the horſe at leaſt would have been ſadly gored. Both the horſe and the knight were within a hair of being trampled upon, when the other knight gave the bull a great cut acroſs the neck, while all the fighters on foot thruſt their daggers, ſome into his mouth and ſome into his eyes. The horſe got up, ran frighted through the croud, and threw ſeveral of them down, while his unlucky rider, who was no great gainer by his tumble, ſtood curſing and ſwearing at the horſe, at the bull, and at himſelf.

Thus ended the maſſacre of thoſe noble animals: a maſſacre encouraged as long as it laſted by a moſt outrageous uproar, and concluded with a moſt thundering clap of univerſal approbation.

What effect theſe cruel ſpectacles (repeated almoſt every Sunday, as I am told) may have upon the morals and religion of this people, better speculatists than myself may determine. To me indeed they appear most brutal and most unchristian. However, they have the sanction of the law of the country; and the government that permits and countenances them, may have reasons for so doing quite out of the reach of my intellects. Therefore, instead of yielding to the temptation of blaming what to me appears very blamable, let me go on with matter of fact, and relate an incident that suspended for about half an hour this horrible entertainment.

The seventh or eighth bull had been just slain and dragg'd out, and the man at the bull's-gate was going to let in another, when the people in the ground-floor-boxes, opposite to that where I was, rose at once one and all with the most hideous shrieks, leapt precipitously into the area, and ran about the place like madmen.

This

This sudden disorder terrified the assembly, and few were those who had any sang-froid left. All wanted to know what was the matter, but the noise of a cataract could not have been traced through the cries of such a multitude. The King and the Queen, the Princesses and Don Pedro raised their hands, fans, and voices, as I could see by the opening of their mouths, but it was a considerable while before a word could be heard about the cause of so violent a commotion. Yet at last the impatience of universal curiosity was satisfied, and a report went round that some people, where the uproar began, had cried out *Earthquake, Earthquake!*

In a country where people have still fresh in their minds the effects of an earthquake, it is no wonder if such a cry, that came at once from several quarters, proved terrifying; and if those who heard it, without giving themselves an instant to reflect, sprung over the barriers into the area, to escape being crush'd by the fall of the edifice.

However, the fact is that not the least shock of an earthquake had been felt by any body. The cry had been raised by a gang of pick-pockets in order to throw the people into confusion, and gain an opportunity of stealing. The scheme took to a wonder. Many men lost their handkerchiefs and many women their caps, not to speak of swords and watches, necklaces and ear-rings.

To frame such a scheme and to carry it into execution so undauntedly as it was carried, appears to me as valiant an atchievement as any of *Orlando*'s. I used often in London to admire the boldness and intrepidity of the British pick-pockets, and thought them the very cleverest in the whole creation. But, away with them! They must not pretend to attempt competition with the heroical pick-pockets of Lusitania.

It

It is needless to tell, that on being apprised of the true cause of that disorder, the whole assembly sat down again in quiet; that the greatest part, who had not been sufferers by it, laughed at the thievish ingenuity; and that a new bull was let loose in the area.

And here is the account concluded of the most important transactions of this afternoon. What follows is merely set down by way of memorandum for my private use, and not worth your reading.

I was told while at the amphitheatre, that one of the King's chariot-horses had lost a shoe; so that his Majesty was obliged to stop in the scorching-sun until another horse was got ready, that he might proceed. I thought it very odd that a King should have servants so careless, and ask'd if he was put in a passion by it; but was answered that he laugh'd it out. A petty gentleman would have storm'd.

This country is one of the hotteſt in Europe; yet its inhabitants are not melted into ſlenderneſs. I never ſaw any where ſo many fat men in one place as I have ſeen to day.

In Liſbon both men and women of the better ſort ſeem to love gaudineſs in dreſs. The Ladies, like thoſe of Tuſcany and other parts of Italy, wear many artificial flowers ſtuck in their hair. It is a pretty faſhion. I ſaw ſeveral beautiful faces to day, and many a pair of brilliant eyes.

Here, as in France and Italy, they have the abſurd cuſtom of dreſſing their children too much. I hate to ſee a little girl with a tupee, and a little ſword at the ſide of a little boy. The Engliſh are not guilty of ſuch folly. In England boys and girls, even when they are ſons and daughters of Earls and Dukes, are never made to look like dwarfiſh men and dwarfiſh women: and this may be the reaſon, that England abounds leſs with fops and coquets than either France or Italy.

LET-

LETTER XX.

Effects of the Earthquake. A City not to be rebuilt in haste.

Lisbon, Sept. 2. 1760.

I Have now visited the ruins of Lisbon at full leisure, and a dreadful indelible image is now imprinted on my mind! But do not expect from me such a description of these ruins, as may even imperfectly convey that image to you. Such a scene of horrible desolation no words are equal to: no words at least that I could possibly put together; and it is ocular inspection only, that can give an adequate idea of the calamity which this city has suffer'd from the ever-memorable earthquake.

As far as I can judge after having walk'd the whole morning and the whole afternoon about these ruins, so much of Lisbon has been destroy'd as would make a town more than twice as great as Turin.

Turin (*a*). In such a space nothing is to be seen but vast heaps of rubbish, out of which arise in numberless places the miserable remains of shatter'd walls and broken pillars.

Along a street which is full four miles in length, scarcely a building stood the shock: and I see by the materials in the rubbish, that many of the houses along that street must have been large and stately, and intermixed with noble churches and other public edifices; nay, by the quantities of marble scatter'd on every side, it plainly appears that one fourth at least of that street was intirely built of marble.

The rage of the earthquake (if I may call it rage) seems to have turned chiefly against

---

(*a*) *Turin, a fortified town in Piedmont, and the King of Sardinia's residence, is little more than a mile in length, taken from the Po-gate to that of Susa, and not quite so much from the King's palace to the New-gate. Lisbon from the Alcantara-gate to the Slave's bagnio is (or was) about four miles, and a mile and a half broad almost throughout.*

against that long street, as almost every edifice on either side is in a manner levelled with the ground: whereas in other parts of the town many houses, churches, and other buildings are left standing; though all so cruelly shattered, as not to be repaired without great expence: Nor is there throughout the whole town a single building of any kind, but what wears visible marks of the horrible concussion.

I cannot be regular in speaking of the various things that struck me to day, but must note them down as well as my crouding thoughts will permit. My whole frame was shaking as I ascended this and that heap of rubbish. Who knows, thought I, but I stand now directly over some mangled body that was suddenly buried under this heap! Some worthy man! Some beautiful woman! Some helpless infant! A whole family perhaps!——Then I came in sight of a ruined

ruined church. Confider its walls giving way! The roof and cupola finking at once, and crufhing hundreds and thoufands of all ages, of all ranks, of all conditions! This was a convent: this was a nunnery: this was a college: this an hofpital! Reflect on whole communities loft in an inftant! The dreadful idea comes round and round with irrefiftible intrufion.

As I was thus rambling over thofe ruins, an aged woman feized me by the hand with fome eagernefs, and pointing to a place juft by: Here, ftranger (faid fhe) do you fee this cellar? It was only my cellar once; but now it is my habitation, becaufe I have none elfe left! My houfe tumbled as I was in it, and in this cellar was I fhut by the ruins for nine whole days. I had perifhed with hunger, but for the grapes that I had hung to the cieling. At the end of nine days I heard people over my head, who were fearching

ing the rubbish. I cried as loud as I could; they removed the rubbish, and took me out.

I asked her what were her thoughts in that dismal situation; what her hopes, what her fears. Fears I had none, said she. I implored the assistance of St. Anthony who was my protector ever since I was born. I expected my deliverance every moment, and was sure of it. But, alas! I did not know what I was praying for! It had been much better for me to die at once! I came out unhurt: but what signifies living a short while longer in sorrow and in want, and not a friend alive! My whole family perished! We were thirteen in all: and now——none but myself!

Hear of another deliverance no less uncommon. A gentleman was going in his calash along a kind of terrace, raised on the brink of an eminence which commands the whole town. The frighten'd mules leap'd down that eminence at the first

first shock. They and the rider were killed on the spot and the calash broken to pieces, and yet the gentleman got off unhurt.

But there would be no end of relating the strange accidents that befel many on that dreadful day. Every body you meet has twenty to tell.

The King had two palaces in Lisbon and they were both destroyed. Yet none of the royal family perished. They were just going from *Lisbon* to *(a) Bellém*, and just in a part of the road where there was no house nigh. Had they stayed a quarter of an hour longer in town, or reached *Bellém* a quarter of an hour sooner, they had probably perished, as the royal palace at *Bellém* was likewise nearly destroyed. King, Queen, Princesses, and all their attendants were obliged to encamp in a garden and in the

neigh-

(a) Bellém *is a town or village about three miles from* Lisbon, *where the King and royal family pass the best part of the year.*

neighbouring fields: and I well remember that the British Envoy who was there at that time, wrote over to his court, that five days after the earthquake he went to *Bellém* to pay his respects to them, but that the Queen had sent him word she could not receive him, as she was under a tent, and in no condition to be seen. Imagine what the misery of the people must have been when even the royal family suffered so much.

Nor must I forget to mention the universal conflagration that followed the earthquake. You know that this misfortune fell out on All-Saints day, at ten o'clock in the morning; that is, when all the kitchen-fires were lighted against dinner time, and all the churches illuminated in honour of the day. The fires in the kitchens and the lights in the churches rolled against the combustible matters that could not fail to be in their way, and the ruined town was presently in a flame. *Lisbon* is furnished with water

by

by-means of aqueducts; but the aqueducts were broken by the concuſſion: ſo that little or no water was at hand. Yet had it been ever ſo plentiful, ſtill the town would not have eſcaped the conflagration, becauſe *(a)* every body ran away to the fields and other open places: and thus more loſs was cauſed by the fire than by the earthquake itſelf, as it conſumed all that people had in their houſes, which might in a good meaſure have been dug out of the ruins if it had not been conſumed by that fire. What a ſpectacle for three hundred thouſand people to ſee their homes burning all at once!

But is it not ſurpriſing, after ſuch an earthquake and ſuch a conflagration, to hear

---

(a) Mr. Clark ſays, that on the firſt ſhaking of the ground the people " throng'd into the churches." How could he believe thoſe who told him this? He ſays alſo, that only " one fourth part" of Liſbon was deſtroyed by the earthquake. He would have ſeen that it was more than two thirds, if he had viſited thoſe ruins. I hope he will excuſe my redreſſing a few more of his miſtakes when I come to ſpeak of Toledo and Madrid.

hear the Portuguese constantly repeat (and they have repeated it every day since) that their city is soon to be built over again, quite regular, quite fine, finer than ever it was? and all this to be effected in a little time? Indeed they give me no very high notion of their common sense when they abandon themselves so much to their fiery imaginations.

They say themselves that, upon a moderate computation, *Lisbon* contained four and twenty thousand houses. Of these no less than two thirds have been levelled to the ground, and the other third was left in no very good condition. However, waving the necessary repairs to that third, and considering only the two that are demolished, how is the rubbish of sixteen thousand houses to be removed, along with that of some hundred of large churches, two royal palaces, and many convents, nunneries, hospitals, and other public edifices? If half the people that have escaped the earthquake, were to be employed in nothing else but in the removal of that immense rubbish, it is not very clear that they would be able to remove it in ten years. Then where are the materials for rebuilding sixteen thousand houses and some hundred of other edifices? Many of those houses were four, five, six, and even seven stories high.

It is true, that the country round abounds with marble enough to build twenty Lisbons. But still, that marble must be cut out of the quarry, must be shaped, must be carried to town. And is all this to be done in a little time? and by people who have lost in the conflagration whatever tools they had?

But they will rebuild the town with bricks for the quicker dispatch. Yet the making millions of millions of bricks (even supposing the proper clay quite at hand) is not the work of a day. And kilns must be erected, and wood must be be got to burn them. But where is that wood, in which I am told the country is far from abounding? And where are the thousands of brick-makers to make those numberless millions of bricks? Yet give them brick-makers, clay, and wood as much as will suffice, where is the lime, the iron, and the other materials?

But where do they actually dwell? some hundred thousands of people surely cannot live in the open air?

This question is soon answered. Many dwell in those houses that were left standing, and rendered habitable again by hasty repairs and by propping them on every side, and many more dwell in numerous wooden huts and cottages which they have hastily built round their ruined town. Clusters of those cottages and huts form various parts of the prospects commanded by my windows. I must add, that many of the poorest sort have shifted the rubbish here and there, have cleared many ground-floor-rooms, and many under-ground-cellars; and there they live, if not with convenience, at leaſt under ſhelter. It is needleſs to ſay that thouſands and thouſands have migrated to other places.

However, the Portugueſe have not been idle, and ever ſince the fatal day have been building apace. But what, beſides the mentioned huts and cottages? What, but an Arſenal: and that ſo very large (as I am told) that there will be no edifice of that kind in the whole world to be compared to it when it is finiſhed with the grand Portico adjoining to it, where merchants are to aſſemble at what they call *change-hours* in England.

This is almoſt the only conſiderable building that has been carried on in Liſbon ever ſince the earthquake; and I will not ſay, that inſtead of a magnificent fabrick it would have been better to build ſome ſcore of good houſes, nor will I remark that ſhips might for a while have been bought ready made, and
mer-

mercantile bufinefs tranfacted at leaft for a few years in an humbler place than the grand Portico; but I cannot help faying, that, if I were allowed to wifh in favour of the poor inhabitants of Lifbon, I would rather fee one of their old ftreets rebuilt, than the grandeft Arfenal: rather fome few ftore-houfes to fecure merchandizes, than a great Portico for their owners to confabulate under. But the people, for whom I could form fuch wifhes, feem to have another way of thinking, and who knows but as foon as that wonderful Arfenal is compleated they fet about to rebuild their inquifition, their cathedral, or fome ftupendous convent?

It feems the prevailing opinion amongft the Portuguefe, that the numbers loft in the ruins of this town, amounted to more than ninety thoufand. But fuppofe they exaggerate by two thirds, as the unhappy are apt to do, ftill a number remains

mains that makes the blood run cold at the thought!

Nor is Lisbon the only place in Portugal that has undergone this woeful visitation. I am told that other towns have suffer'd still more in proportion. One in particular called *Setúbal* was so perfectly destroyed that not one person escaped!

But I will quit this subject. It fills one with sadness to no manner of purpose.

LETTER XXI.

The laying of a fundamental stone. A patriarchal pomp. Pied-horses.

Lisbon, Sept. 3, 1760.

I Have seen the King of Portugal and his whole court in great gala, this being a memorable anniversary, as his Majesty this day three years narrowly escaped being treacherously murdered by the Duke d'Aveiro and his associates.

That

That was a bloody transaction, and no less incomprehensible than bloody. It is not easily conceived that the Duke should be prompted and sollicited to take away his Sovereign's life by many relations and friends, and by the whole body of the Portuguese jesuits: that so execrable a conspiracy should require the concurrence of many, when at last it was to be executed by a few: that the dreadful secret should be entrusted with men and women, masters, and servants, ecclesiastics and lay-men, and not one out of some hundred should be tempted by hope, impelled by terror, or induced by a better motive to discover it in time: that such a secret should so faithfully be kept by the whole gang of the conspirators as not even to be suspected by so wary and suspicious a government! all this is quite incomprehensible. But let us come to the gala.

In that village called *Bellém*, already named, a wooden edifice has been erected within these few days upon the very spot where his Majesty was fired at by the murderers.

This edifice is eighty of my steps in length and five and twenty broad. The inside of it was hung with a kind of red serge striped and fringed with a tinsel-lace. In the middle of it was placed an altar gloriously adorned. Facing the altar there were two pews, one for the King and the other for the Queen, besides a smaller for *Don Bastian Joseph de Carvalho* secretary of State. Under the Queen's pew there was a kind of throne for *Cardinal Saldanha* the patriarch. The remainder of the place was occupied pell-mell by the nobility of the kingdom, foreign ministers, and all strangers well dress'd. The patriarch's attendants however, as well as the musicians, had some benches to themselves.

As the day proved inexpressibly hot, the doors and windows of the edifice were kept open during the ceremony, so that the numberless spectators from with-

out

out enjoyed it near as well as those within.

About nine o'clock Secretary *Carvalho* made his appearance preceded by many gentlemen, many servants, a drummer, and a trumpeter, all on horseback. He was alone in a coach drawn by six grey horses, attended by two grooms on foot, one on each side of the coach, and by five and twenty of the King's horse-guards.

He had scarcely alighted and got to his pew, when behold the Patriarch! Excepting the Pope, there is no ecclesiastic in the world that is ever surrounded with so great a pomp as this Patriarch. But his revenue, they say, amounts to thirty thousand pounds sterling, and so he may well afford it.

Two coaches full of priests began the march. Then followed fifty of his Eminence's servants walking two and two in blue liveries trimm'd with a crimson silk-lace, all uncover'd, all well powder'd,
and

and all wearing large cloaks that reached the ground. A prieſt on horſeback went before them, holding up a ſilver-croſs fix'd on the top of a ſtick ſilver'd over. Then followed ſeven coaches. The two firſt were occupied by his Eminence's ecclefiaſtical officers. In the third was the Patriarch himſelf with his maſter of the ceremonies who kept his back to the horſes. Two prieſts walk'd on foot, one on this ſide of the coach and the other on the other. Each bore in his hand an umbrello of crimſon-velvet, fring'd round with gold. They were both ſo tall, that they put me in mind of *Don Fracaſſa* and *Don Tempeſta* in the poem of *Ricciardetto*. The coach of the Patriarch both within and without was lined with blue velvet, gilt and painted very much and very well. Then followed his ſtate-coach empty, ſo rich and ſo fine that Queen Semiramis would not have thought it unworthy of herſelf. Then three more coaches full again of officers; I mean eccleſiaſtics all,

even

even some of the fifty that walk'd in procession. Each of the four first coaches was drawn by six pied-horses; that is, horses streak'd with black and white, which, it seems, are not so uncommon in Portugal and Spain, as they are in other countries. They all galop'd; but their galopping was so close and short, that the attendants on foot could keep up with it, though they walked with great slowness and solemnity. The three next coaches, instead of horses, had six mules each, much finer than any I ever saw in Italy. The Patriarch was dress'd in his great pontificals. And how did he look? In Petrarch's words

Stavasi tutto umile in tanta gloria.

While this noble procession was advancing towards the wooden edifice, more than twenty other coaches, each drawn by six mules, appeared from several parts, and in them were the dignitaries and canons of Lisbon-Cathedral. They all alighted at the door of the edifice and walk'd walk'd partly to the right and partly to the left of the Patriarch's throne. I had quitted my chaise and borrowed *Batiste*'s horse, that I might look at all the great folks with better convenience. Was I pleased with so magnificent a show, or was I disgusted by so vain a parade? I was pleased, because I am no morose philosopher. Such sights are naturally delightful, and I never found my account in counteracting nature. I overheard an Englishman damn the puppet-show, and thought him ill-natured or discontented.

The King then came in a coach and six, the horses black and white like the Patriarch's, surrounded with four and twenty of his horse-guards. Don Pedro was with him. The Queen followed immediately with her four daughters and an elderly lady, all in one coach, with four more coaches, two before and two behind, full of ladies, all coaches and six. Her Majesty was environed by a troop of her own horse-guards, who are much

better

better dress'd than the King's, and, as I am told, all foreigners, chiefly Irish, Scotch, and Germans. She and the Princesses were most magnificently dress'd, wearing most ample hoops, their heads, necks, breasts, arms, waists, and feet glittering with jewels. The Princesses have very fine shapes, fine complections, and the finest eyes that can be seen. One of them (I think the third, but am not sure) as far as my wretched eyes could judge at the distance of seven or eight yards, is a striking beauty. I was pleased to see them so lively and hopping out of the coach with so much nimbleness.

In the pew they all kneeled for a moment, except the Queen who sat down and fell a-reading and kissing the leaves of her book. As she did this more than forty times in a few minutes I ask'd what was the meaning of that kissing, and was answer'd that it was her Majesty's custom to kiss the name of God, of our blessed Lady, and of all Saints and Angels in any book

book that she reads. This singularity brought to my mind an English Philosopher (Mr. *Boyle*, if I do not mistake) who used to bow whenever God's name was mentioned.

The Queen lay'd down her book and a great *Te Deum* was sung with much noise of music. The *Te Deum* was follow'd by the litanies.

The King then got up, and attended by Don Pedro, Secretary Carvalho, and some other gentlemen of his court, descended into a kind of hole about breast-high, where silver-shovels, silver-hammers, and other implements of masonry had been placed before hand with stones, brick, and mortar. His Majesty put some gold and silver medals at the bottom of that hole and cover'd them with a quadrangular stone; then both he and his attendants took up their shovels, and fell a covering that stone with bricks and mortar, beating the bricks with the hammers from time to time, as they were directed

directed by a gentleman, who, I suppose, is the King's architect. And thus was placed the fundamental stone of a most noble church, which is to be forthwith erected there by way of *Ex-voto* to our blessed Lady for the miraculous deliverance the King obtained through her means from the blunderbusses of the Duke d'Aveiro and the other assassins.

In a few minutes the business of laying the stone was over, during which I could not help wondering at some vulgar women who, looking through one of the windows, laughed immoderately at the masons, probably because they were somewhat aukward at their new trade, and this discomposed a little the gravity of the by-standers. Yet no body took any particular notice of their impertinence.

The King and his company returned to their places, and as soon as they were seated, the Patriarch quitting his throne stood up to the altar and celebrated a
high

high mafs affifted by his dignitaries and canons with the ceremonies obferved by the Cardinals to the Pope, when his Holinefs officiates in the moft folemn functions. During the mafs the muficians play'd and fung moft glorioufly. The King has a good many in his fervice, and, what is remarkable, more than forty Italians, partly fingers and partly players upon feveral inftruments.

The mafs lafted a full hour, and was followed by the patriarchal benediction, after which the company broke up and every body went home tired and fatigued. The heat without was great, as the fun fhone very bright, but within was quite intolerable.

At fome diftance from the edifice there was all the while a foot battalion upon guard, the common men ill-dreffed and ill-comb'd. They were not allow'd to fire as they do in Italy upon the like occafions; and this I thought judicioufly ordered, as they would have frighted the

horfes

horses and mules, and made them prance over the multitude: and I was also pleased to see several officers repeatedly command the horse-guards to keep close and ride softly, that no body might be hurt.

The day before yesterday at the Amphitheatre I had seen a good number of ladies. To-day I saw many more at the wooden edifice, and had reason to be pleased at the sight in both places. To-day especially they were all richly dress'd, thick-set with jewels, and many of them very handsome. They are in general much fairer than one would expect in so hot a latitude, which makes me suppose that they take care not to go much in the sun. Almost all have open countenances and simpering looks. A good contrast to their men, whose skins are rather swarthy, and whose faces are sullen and grave, even when they attempt to smile, which they do often enough. The salutation of men to ladies consists in a fhort and quick genuflexion, fuch as we make in Italy to our beft *Madona*'s when we are in a hurry. But this compliment the ladies fcarcely return with a nod, efpecially to inferiors. The gentlemen embrace each other with great refpect when they meet, and kifs each other's left fhoulder.

I am told that no body in Lifbon is allowed to have horfes to his coach, chaife, or other vehicle, except the Royal Family, Minifters of State, Patriarch, foreign Minifters, and a few others. The reft make ufe of mules. Portugal, they fay, does not abound in horfes, and the Portuguefe are obliged to fmuggle many out of Spain, whence the fale is forbidden under fevere penalties.

Female drefs is no where variated fo much as amongft the low women in this country. Some hide themfelves under veils of different ftuffs and colours, and fome appear quite uncovered. Some have their hair plaited up, fome let it flow down

down their shoulders, and some confine it in one or more hanging tresses. Some have coifures after the French manner, and some wear hats after the English. Many adorn their heads with ribbonds, and many with natural or artificial flowers. The earthquake has been the cause of so great a variety on this particular. As it has deprived the greatest part of them of their wearing apparel, they dress now as well as they can, and have no prevalent or national fashion.

LETTER XXII.

Another fine Prospect. Rhyme and blank-verse. Heavenly life at the Jeronimites. Banks of the Tagus again. Sowing of Salt.

Lisbon, Sept. 5, 1760.

AS I was looking yesterday into a Portuguese book, I took notice that it was printed *en Lisboa Occidental*.

What means, said I, this *Occidental Lisbon?* Is there any other besides this?

No such thing, quoth the French bookseller. Some *Lusitanian* Literati affirm, that the ancient *Olisipo* stood on the opposite side of the river, because an ancient inscription was once found there in which *Olisipo* is mentioned. Upon this scanty foundation and to make a parade of erudition, some of them bestow that epithet of *Occidental* on this town, without considering, that, were their conjectures true, still there would be no room for that distinction, as no book was ever printed *en Lisboa Oriental*.

How far the bookseller is right or wrong I cannot determine. However, thought I, I will go and visit the opposite side of the river, and see if I can find out any thing worth a paragraph in a letter. A place suspected by the learned to have been *Lisbon,* well deserves a visit.

In consequence of this resolution this morning early I got into a boat with *Batiste, sifte*, and failed away to the other side of the *Tagus*.

The bank of the river on that side I found a great deal higher than this. It is a perfect mountain. But where I landed there is no house nor room to build any. I saw a path that leads up to the top of the hill, and clamber'd up. The path is craggy and difficult enough. On the summit there are two villages, one called *Castillo*, the other *Almada*.

Castillo has nothing that is remarkable, except the new ruins of an old-fashion'd castle, perhaps moorish, which probably gave name to the village. It is situated on a cliff made in the form of a sugar-loaf, and I am told that it was decay'd and uninhabited even before the earthquake reduced it in its present condition.

At *Almada*, which is about a musket-shot from *Castillo*, I enter'd a small Dominican convent, whose cloister-walls are incrusted with tiles painted blue, and so very neat and clean, that the very looking on them is cooling in this hot weather. The church which belong'd to the convent was thrown down by the first shock of the earthquake, and the shattered bodies of about twenty men and six times more women were dug out of its ruins. The convent stood the concussion, so that none of the friars perished but that one who was saying mass in the church.

From the windows on the west-side you have a prospect which excels even that of *Mount Edgecombe* in Devonshire, as from thence you have Lisbon full in your eyes: then *Bellêm, Cascáes, St. Julian*, and all the villages, castles, fortifications, and other buildings along the river down to the sea, with an immense landscape surrounding all this, bounded on one side by the *Rock of Lisbon* already mentioned, and in other places by other hills whose names I know not. The prospect from the east-windows is likewise very fine, though not so striking, as

it

it confists only of a long range of hills covered with vineyards interfperfed with numberlefs fruit-trees of every kind, efpecially oranges and lemons, with houfes and cottages from place to place. Charming *Almada!* though not embellifhed by any better building than the Dominican convent, certainly becaufe there is no means of reaching fo high a place but on foot or on a mule. Both *Almada* and *Caftillo* were little lefs than levelled to the ground by the earthquake.

After having enjoy'd the profpects to my fatisfaction, I rolled down the craggy path again, got to the boat and went to fee an Englifh hofpital which ftands a little lower down on the fame fide of the river, and at the foot of the hill, where the ground juts out a little into the water. But there I faw nothing worth notice, except the Phyfician to the hofpital, an old and ill-bred gentleman; perhaps rendered ill-bred by jealoufy, as he has had the weaknefs at feventy to marry a pretty Portuguese girl of eighteen. He look'd very cross when he saw me enter the garden of the hospital, because the young lady was then in it gathering some fruit. As he had answer'd rather uncivilly some civil question I had put to him, I was tempted to make him fret a little by addressing her and begging a grape out of her basket. However I resisted the temptation, as I reflected that I may myself possibly be guilty of the same folly at his age, if ever I reach it. Therefore, after having taken a tour of the garden, I made him a bow, got again into the boat, and sailed up the river, still on the same side, to the house of one *O'Neal*, an Irish wine-merchant, whose ample cellars are worth seeing.

I found Mr. *O'Neal* quite the reverse of the Physician. As he saw me in a heat, he made me drink some of his best wine, gave me a bisket, offer'd any other refreshment I chose, and was even kind in the same way to *Batiste* and my boat-

boatmen, nor would he (*a*) accept of any pecuniary equivalent.

The houſe Mr. *O'Neal* has there, is defended from the encroachments of the river by a ſtrong mole of large flat ſtones. From that mole I enjoyed the ſight of two Negros ſwimming and playing gambols in the water. Had I never ſeen blacks before, I had miſtaken them for ſome particular ſpecies of fiſh. They ſprang out of the water and wheel'd upon it, as tumblers do upon firm ground. For a few reis I made them ſing ſeveral ſongs in their *Moſambique* language, of which I comprehend nothing but that they were in rhyme. I wiſhed myſelf a muſician, only to take down the tunes of what they ſung, though very ſimple with regard to harmony.

Several writers both of Italy and of England have affirmed, that rhyme is

a

(*a*) *I recommend him to thoſe of my Engliſh readers who deal in Portugal-wine. I am poſitive he deſerves cuſtomers for his kindneſs to thirſty people, even when they are perfectly unknown to him, as was my caſe.*

a monkish invention; but I think them widely mistaken. It is not to be supposed that the Africans were taught rhyming by Missionaries, who have other business when in those regions than that of teaching rhyme or blank-verse to the natives. I heard once in *Venice* some Arabian songs which were in rhyme, and there is a French account of Arabia (wrote by a traveller whose name I cannot at present recollect) in which some poetry of that wandering nation is preserved, all in rhyme. One *Gages* an Englishman (who suggested to *Cromwell* the scheme of taking *Jamaica* from the Spaniards) in a printed account of *America* has given us an old *Mexican* song (words and musick) which is in rhyme, and composed long before *Columbus* was born. These and a multitude of other such reasons have convinced me, that rhyme is no monkish invention, but one of the natural essentials of the poetry of all nations, ancient as well as modern, *Greek* and *Latin* only excepted.

ed, whose verses had feet instead of rhymes. It is therefore blank-verse that is to be considered as not natural to poetry, and to be deemed an invention, as it really was, and not a very ancient one.

But let me take my leave of the courteous *O'Neal*, and cross the *Tagus* again as I go down the stream. I was set on shore at *Bellèm*, where I enter'd a most scurvy inn for a bad dinner. Then I visited a famous convent of Jeronimites; an order we have not in *Piedmont*, and not very common in other parts of western *Italy*.

The church of that convent is actually repairing, as its roof was thrown down by the earthquake. The scaffolding erected for this purpose did not permit me to see much of it. I only could see that it is one of the largest I ever saw, built with fine marble of various colours, and adorned with the richest altars. The architecture of the whole edifice was
originally

originally gothic, but some parts of the convent are so no longer. The two galleries or cloisters which run one over the other, contain a number of statues, some of the most popular saints, and some of saints whose names and character I am not acquainted with, though the legend was my favourite book when I was a boy.

There are a hundred and thirty massfriars in this convent, and I don't know how many lay-ones. Their cells are very good rooms. Those who are lodged on the water-side, may from their windows enjoy the sight of the ships incessantly going up and down the river. The back apartments command a spacious garden and a piece of uneven ground, wall'd in and full of olive-trees.

Amongst those trees are several little cells and chapels belonging to several paultry sinners of low condition who have repented, and are allowed to live there in perfect idleness; which way of consuming time is by them termed *Vida celeste*, a hea-

a heavenly life; nor is the appellation much amiss in my opinion, if it be taken in the poetical sense; as the privilege of living without working, is really the chief blessing of this life. They subsist upon mere accidental alms, of which they have plenty by the intercession of *St. Jerome,* who like them lived in a cell or cave in the midst of a desart, and of course makes it his particular business that his followers be abundantly supplied.

As this convent is of royal foundation, you may be sure that the friars in it have a better chance for their dinners than casual charities. They live very comfortably and have no other obligation but that of praying some hour every day for their original benefactor and his successors. This duty they are forced to perform regularly, whether they are inclined to it or not. But the pious founders of religious houses never thought that frequent and regular praying must prove a hardship, and always took it for granted that

that a number of men well fed, warmly dress'd, and conveniently lodged, would never repine to solicit heaven for their deliverance out of purgatory. They supposed that when worldly cares were removed, devotion would regularly take possession of the heart, and I wish that they had never been mistaken.

The church there, was formerly (and may be so still for what I know) the burial-place of the Kings and Queens of Portugal. I am told there are in it several of their sepulchral monuments; but I could not see them because of the scaffolding.

One of the *Padres* who showed me the place, encouraged me to eat of the fine grapes of the garden, and I can tell you that you have scarce any so good in Italy. Their figs are also excellent. They have many *Brasilian* plants in that garden, particularly that called *Banana*. They all grow in the open air, and with no particular culture that I could see. By this

this you may judge of the heat of this climate.

As I failed up again to *Lisbon*, I enjoyed again from the boat the fine prospect I had from the packet on my arrival. It is really as enchanting as can possibly be conceived. By *Bellêm* there is a noble structure called *Paço de Vaca (the Palace of the Gow*, an odd name) where the King's horses are educated for the manage. It is embellished with busts and statues, partly placed in niches and partly on the ridge of its walls. Then the palace called the *Vice-queen*'s of the Indies; that of *Marquis Gingez*; that of the *French Ambassador*; that of the *late Patriarch*; that of the *present Patriarch*; that of the *Secretary of State* for the marine department; the fortress called *La Jonqueira*; the palace that was occupied by *Cardinal Acciajoli* the *Pope's Nuncio*, lately driven out of Portugal in a very abrupt and rough manner: then that of *Count Ribeira*; that of *Don Emanuel*,

uncle

uncle to his prefent majefty; that of *Secretary Carvalho*, and another which has been degraded to *a jail* for ftate-criminals, not far from which ftood heretofore that of the *Duke d'Aveiro*, which is now nearly demolifhed, purfuant to the fentence that was paft on its mafter.

All thefe and other ftructures, whofe names I have forgotten, would not misbecome the nobleft of our Italian towns. They adorn the intermediate fpace between *Bellém* and *Lifbon*, nor has the earthquake damaged them much. Yet they are not the only decoration of that part of the fhore. There is befides a vaft number of houfes, as I faid already, all white, with their windows and windowfhutters or lattices painted green. When the ftones of the *D'Aveiro* palace are removed (which, by the bye, is done carefully that they may not be fpoilt, as they are worth preferving) and the fpot is made level, falt is to be fowed upon it, that it may never bear any grafs: which

to

to me seems a very unjust punishment inflicted upon a poor piece of ground that certainly had no part in the crime of its owner: and after the sowing of that supposed enemy to fertility, a high marble-column is to be erected in the centre of that spot with an inscription upon it, to perpetuate the infamy of that bloody traitor, whose character (if I am not misinformed) was a hateful mixture of the grossest ignorance and the most brutal pride. Men will determine according to their different dispositions; and he had a punctilious abhorrence to that sort of honour which is at present generally disregarded throughout Europe, and thoroughly exploded from France, where even the greatest Lords are ambitious of being a-kin to a certain sort of women.

As I was coming back towards evening, I took the *King-George-Packet* in my way, drank a bumper with my seafaring gentlemen, and had a touch at the bag-pipe. They have promised to come and dine with me before they set sail for *Falmouth*.

LETTER XXIII.

A specimen of poetical style. An aqueduct.

Lisbon, Sept. 6, 1760.

UPON the report of others I have in a former letter mentioned the Arsenal they are actually building here. But I have been this day an ocular admirer myself of its amplitude, and will venture to say that if the smallest closet in it was turned into a ball-room, we might have a dance in it of all the giants and giantesses ever dream'd of by the noble *Don Quixote* whenever the moon was at the fullest. Indeed when it is finished (if ever it is) the poets of this country will be justly entitled to say in their usual emphatic strain, that *in the new-built metropolis of the Lusitanian empire (true and astonishing abridgment of puissant Assiria, dreaded Macedonia, scientific Greece, and all-conquering Rome) there*

is

is so vast, so beautiful, and so costly an edifice, as may without exaggeration be compared to the mountainous temple of the chaste Ephesian Goddess, to the unmeasurable mausoleum of the faithful and sorrowful Artemisa, to the incomprehensible Naumachian structures of the most magnificent though most blood-thirsty Dioclesian, and even to those terror-striking pyramids erected on the extensive shores of the ever-fertile Ethiopian river, whose ponderosity has made the Egyptian provinces groan for centuries and centuries, and whose sharp-pointed summits pierce the far-spreading darkness that environs the adamantine throne of great Jupiter's resplendent queen, and seem to challenge to mortal and everlasting war the most distant, most numerous, and most unpropitious constellations.

I will not say that this manner of writing is adopted by all the modern poets of Portugal: but amongst that infinity of sonnets just published on the laying of the fundamental stone of the church, which is to be dedicated to the *Nossa Senhora da Liberaçaom*, a good many ran very much in this style: and I dare to say, that if this encomium on the new Arsenal was to be turned into a Portuguese ode, it would not meet here with universal disapprobation.

To be serious, this Arsenal is a huge fabrick, and, in the opinion of many, quite disproportionate to the use intended. However, there is never any great harm in public edifices being too large, because those parts in them which are superfluous one way, may easily be made serviceable another. Thus many rooms in this may be turned upon occasion into granaries, store-rooms, quarters for soldiers, hospitals, and other such receptacles, of which there are never enough in great capital cities.

This edifice I visited this morning: but I went to see another of another kind in the afternoon, which surpasses it by far in point of bulk as well as magnificence.

I mean

I mean the *Aqueduct* in the valley of *Alcántara*, by which *Lisbon* is supplied with almost all the water that is used by the inhabitants.

That valley is sunk between two rocky and barren declivities. The Aqueduct for about a quarter of a mile, which is the breadth of the valley, runs transversely over it, from the summit of the western declivity to the opposite summit of the eastern. A long range of square pillars supports it: and to give you an idea of these pillars, it is enough to say, that one of their sides measures near twelve, and the other near thirteen times the length of my sword, which was the only instrument I had to take such measures; and the space between the two middle-most pillars is such, both in breadth and height, that a fifty-gun ship with her sails spread might pass through without obstruction. However, all the pillars are not of equal dimensions with the two central. They grow lower and lower,

lower, and the spaces betwixt them diminish gradually on either side the valley, as the ground gradually rises on either side.

The pillars support an architrave whose middle is formed into a canal, through which the water runs: and there is room enough left for three or four men to walk abreast along the architrave on each side the canal which is vaulted the whole length, and adorned from space to space with *Lucarnes* made in the form of little temples, each of which has a door or aperture large enough for a man to get at the water and clean the bottom of the canal in case of necessity.

The whole of this immense fabrick is of fine white marble dug out of a quarry not a musket-shot distant: and I am told that about a league further off there are some other parts of it which have their share of grandeur, though by no means comparable to what is seen in this valley. The earthquake had spoilt it in two or three

three places: but the damage proved inconsiderable and was easily remedied. And indeed I wonder not if it withstood the shocks. A concussion violent enough to effect its destruction, would shatter the whole kingdom of Portugal.

When a man has once seen such a structure as the Aqueduct of *Alcántara*, there is no danger of his ever forgetting it, as it is the nature of grand objects to force remembrance. As long as I live I shall preserve the image of it, along with that of the valley which is rendered so conspicuous by it.

However, if there was no such thing as that glorious Aqueduct in that valley, still I should never forget the valley itself, because of an adventure I met in it of a pretty singular kind. But the visit to the two edifices, which was performed on foot and in the heat of the day, has fatigued me so much, that the account of it must be delay'd till to-morrow.

LETTER XXIV.

Lapidation performed in a valley. Good Mothers.

Lisbon, Sept. 7, 1769.

WHILE I am waiting for the barber I may as well tell my adventure of yesterday in the Valley of *Alcántara*.

After having fully satisfied my curiosity with regard to the noble Aqueduct, we turned back the way we went. But as we ascended one side of the valley we met with five or six men wrapp'd up to their noses in their ample cloaks, which it is the custom here to wear both winter and summer. They pull'd off their hats, and we pull'd off ours, because this is another custom of the people here, to give each other this token of respect whenever they meet about the country. But the cloak'd fellows had not gone twenty yards from us, when, turning suddenly

suddenly back, they began to hurl stones at us with such precipitance and fury, as could not be described by the best *Balearick* poet of *Majorca*.

What is the meaning of this? cried I to my landlord Mr. *Kelly*.

Run for your life was the answer: and he took to his heels with such celerity as if he had utterly forgot that he is full seventy.

What could I do on seeing myself thus abandoned by my auxiliary troops? Spare me the mortification of owning, that I made my retreat with as much haste as I could, and thus baffled the cruel intention of the villains, and the fatal consequence that might have ensued from that unexpected lapidation.

And now tell me, dear brothers, the motive that induced them to treat me and my fellow-walker in so barbarous a manner?

Sir, says *Kelly* with an air of triumph, will you still laugh at me when I tell you

that

that you tarry too late at the English Coffee-house? Upon my soul, one night or other you will see what it is in this country to come home at eleven and alone!

But here is the barber, and I must not make him wait.

A Postscript *in the evening*. My Landlord has given you a hint that I am so imprudent as to spend an hour or two in the evening at a coffee-house, where all manner of strangers resort, especially of the English nation. Not one of those strangers have I as yet heard speak favourably of the Portuguese. On the contrary they all join to paint them in the blackest colours, and would fain persuade any new comer, that this is the most unpolished, most inhospitable, and most hateful nation under the sun. But notwithstanding their invectives I was until yesterday-evening rather inclined to a contrary opinion, as such assertions

squared

squared not with my first cursory observations. I had taken notice that the Portuguese are very respectful to each other, and quick to bow to any body they meet out of a croud: that they are enthusiastic admirers of women, and treat them with a pleasing mixture of obsequiousness and gallantry: that they have a strong musical turn, and are fond of spending the first part of the night in singing and playing about the streets; nor had I seen any thing deserving censure in their general behaviour at church.

These obvious characteristics of the Portuguese I thought rather incompatible with treachery and unprovoked inhumanity; besides that I know enough of mankind to be tolerably acquainted with their vile antipathies and with their readiness severally to abuse and depreciate their neighbours upon the slightest provocation, and often upon no provocation at all. No nation upon record has yet found grace before another, and each is

thought

thought detestable by the rest. This universal brutality in the gross of mankind, made me unwilling to believe the many bad things repeatedly told me of the Portuguese; and I should have persisted unshaken in my incredulity, had it not been for that iniquitous lapidation, which, I think, has given me ground enough to credit in a good measure the uniform accusations brought against them by all men of other nations that have resided here.

You may possibly upbraid me still for my seeming facility in adopting this harsh opinion, and insist that my motive is still very slight and equivocal. And indeed I really wish I could persuade myself that the low part of this nation is not a mass of villains, and that the fellows in that Valley are by no means to be considered as the legal representatives of their peers, but only as a groupe of rogues who met unluckily together by mere chance.

But

But that I may put you in a condition to judge adequately of this matter, I muſt alſo tell you, that yeſterday likewiſe, as we were going to ſee that Aqueduct, a parcel of children followed us at ſome diſtance in a moſt clamorous manner, and loaded us with ſuch execrable contumelies, as generally ſurpaſs the abilities of children in other countries.

The impotent inſult of thoſe growing raſcals, I ſhould have forgot as ſoon as it was over, but for an ugly circumſtance that attended it. The circumſtance was, that ſeveral women, on hearing that ſudden vociferation, ruſh'd out from ſeveral quarters, and joining with the perverſe children, encouraged them to give us more and more of their abuſive language, and made them follow us much longer than they would otherwiſe have done if they had been left to themſelves. Some of thoſe women were apparently mothers to ſome of thoſe children; and what judgment can a man paſs upon a nation,

when

when he sees mothers abetting their boys and girls in their aversion to strangers, and fortifying them in their barbarous brutality?

Thus far have I already push'd my obfervations on the low part of the people within this town. I am willing to believe that the higher sort are quite the reverse, and that they know politeness and humanity full as well as the higher sort of all other European nations, though I have not forgot the stupid haughtiness and forbidding look of the two gentlemen and the friar in the box at the Amphitheatre. But whatever I may believe, don't you begin to think that Portugal is rather too much in the neighbourhood of Africa?

LETTER XXV.

Good nuns. A scheme for rendering girls still more amiable. Heroism of a young Lady.

Lisbon, Sept. 8. 1760.

THIS morning I made a visit to one of those many religious houses that are maintained in several parts of this kingdom at the King's expence. It is call'd *the English Nunnery*, because no girl is admitted in it but what is born a subject of England. Any such girl, either left destitute in this country by parents unsuccessful in trade, or willing to come from the British Isles to devote herself in this country to chastity and confinement, may make sure of a livelihood in that Nunnery; and the veil once taken, she needs not to fear the approaches of real want as long as her soul and body will keep each other company.

The

The number of the nuns there amounts to little more than twenty, and it is the chief anxiety of this little community to keep the number full, that the Government may not, in case of too many vacancies, take upon itself to fill them with Portuguese maidens, which the English women apprehend would create separate interests, and cause such feuds and parties amongst them, as they have hitherto been strangers to ever since the first foundation.

Animated by this rare species of terrour, the poor things set their brains upon the utmost stretch whenever death deprives their community of a member, and all efforts are unanimously made towards the raising of a recruit. With this distant view, you cannot conceive how prettily they flatter all their visitors, especially those of their own sex! They keep besides a large epistolary correspondence with their friends and acquaintance

in

In *England* and *Ireland*, by which means they have not failed as yet to obtain the desired supply.

Whoever can speak English, no matter whether Catholic or Protestant, has a kind of right to visit them at any time of the day; and all their visitors are used by them with such an endearing kindness, that their parlatory is in a manner never empty from morning till night. The poor things are liberal to every body of chocolate, cakes, and sweet-meats, and will take much pains with their needles or otherwise to enlarge the number of those visitors, and allure them to frequent calls.

Nuns in all countries are soft and obliging speakers; but these are certainly the softest and most obliging that ever fell in my way. Never was I told in a year so many pretty and tender words as this morning in half an hour. On my apprising them of my country, they expatiated on the immense goodness of Cardinal *Acciaioli* and the gentlemen of his court, who did them the honour of seeing them often. No nation, in their opinion, is so good as the Italian, none so witty, and none so wise. In short, not a syllable issued out at their lips but what was dictated by modesty and meekness, humility and benevolence; and I will positively see them as often as I can while I stay here, because it is impossible not to be pleased with their converse, though one is perfectly conscious that they make it a study to treat every body with this gentleness of language and blandishment of manners. They certainly give you no reason for harbouring the least suspicion to their disadvantage, and their virtue is to all appearance without the least alloy: but were they in reality quite different from what they appear (which I am thoroughly persuaded is not the case), still the strong appearance of their innocence and goodness is irresistibly attracting, and the holy simplicity of their

their behaviour can never fail of making a friend of every man who is once introduced to their acquaintance, though ever so much aware of their flattery.

The King, as I said, allows them such a sum as enables them to find themselves in victuals, linen, and raiment. Thus they are freed from the anxiety of procuring the chief neceſſaries of life. Yet life, even by recluſe women, cannot be paſſed very comfortably with mere neceſſaries, and ſome addition is wanting to keep it from ſtagnating. Thoſe minute ſuperfluities, which the French call *douceurs*, ſo indiſpenſibly required to render exiſtence ſupportable, are left intirely to their induſtry; and theſe they procure partly by work and partly by making trifling preſents, which are often return'd with liberality. Theſe are the two means by which they furniſh themſelves with that chocolate ſo plentifully diſtributed at their parlatory to their inceſſant viſitors, and with thoſe other petty things that alleviate the natural hardneſs of their condition. Some of them have ſmall penſions paid them by their relations and friends, and whatever is got by one, is kindly ſhared by the whole ſiſterhood.

As the reputation of this little community was never ſullied in the leaſt ever ſince their eſtabliſhment (and I am told that this is not quite the caſe with the Portugueſe nunneries) is it not aſtoniſhing that no Portugueſe parent ever thinks of ſending his daughter amongſt them as a boarder and by way of giving her a true maidenly education ? A daughter thus placed would amongſt other advantages have that of learning a foreign language very well worth learning; and nothing contributes ſo much to enlarge the ſphere of our ideas, and to render a young woman amiable, as the knowledge of languages. Yet, few are the Portugueſe, as I am told, who care for ſuch an ornament in their daughters, or even

in

in themselves, excepting those of the highest quality; and they have besides a particular antipathy to the language of England, as the notion prevails amongst them, that there is no book in that language but what is against religion; nor does their inquisition allow of the importation of any for fear of heresy: and it was not without contest and bribery that I saved the few in my trunk from confiscation at the custom-house.

The visiting of the *English Nunnery* has brought a scheme into my mind which I shall cherish long, and put in execution as soon as I can. Let me but be rich enough, and I will have four Nunneries in *Turin*, and endow them with a revenue equal to the maintenance of twenty nuns in each. One of them shall be filled with Florentine women, one of French, one of Spanish, and one of English.

I will take it for granted that when my Nunneries are erected, endowed, and filled with proper inhabitants, my countrymen will have senfe enough to send their little girls to them for education; and by a refidence of about two years in each Nunnery, all the girls in *Piedmont* will be able to fpeak four languages, befides their own; which will certainly render them upon the whole the moſt lovely fet of maidens in Europe.

But as I am not for turning pretty girls into nuns, I intend to make it the fundamental law of my Nunneries, that none of the nuns fhall be young and handfome. It will probably not prove very difficult to procure out of each refpective country one fcore of elderly maids or widows to fill them at firſt, and to keep fucceffively the number quite complete; nor do I intend to fubject them to the auftere rule of keeping always within doors. They fhall have a number of holidays to walk or ride out with their pupils, and be allowed all forts of diverfions becoming a fet of exemplary matrons.

This

This scheme I am confident you will think quite patriotick, and well worth taking place any where. But setting it aside until a properer time, let me tell you a story of *Lady Hill* (the present Abbess of the *English Nunnery*) which really deserves to be saved from oblivion.

This Lady took the veil there, because, like the rest of her sisterhood, (as I suppose) her circumstances did not permit a more agreeable choice: but soon after having made profession, a good estate in *Ireland* was vacated by a relation that died intestate, and of course devolved upon her by right of consanguinity.

To get the estate without going to *Ireland* herself, was thought difficult and subject to much delay. Her Abbess therefore represented her case to the Patriarch, who alone could dispense with her vow of constant confinement; and the Patriarch (not a rigid bigot it seems) upon a simple promise of return gave her leave to secularize her dress and depart.

She did so; arrived in *Ireland*; produced her title; took possession; and found herself at once in a condition to live in ease and even splendour in her native country.

The temptation of staying where one is, you will allow to be nearly irresistible in such a case, especially when you are additionally told, that she was not yet three and twenty, and handsome enough. However, if she was tempted, she was tempted in vain, for she sold the estate as speedily as she could, and, faithful to her vow and promise, hasten'd back to the Nunnery with the money, which she laid out in such a manner as to contribute much to the ease and convenience of her beloved community.

This was done by a woman! This superiority to worldly pleasure, and this fidelity to an onerous engagement, was found in a female breast! Would any friar in similar circumstances have behaved so nobly and have returned to his less heavy fetters after so lucky an escape? This question I will not answer for the honour of my own sex. I will only conclude the story of Lady *Hill*, with telling you that her companions, struck with admiration as well as gratitude, chose her immediately for their superior, and never after ceased to pay her the veneration so undoubtedly due to her unshaken virtue.

LETTER XXVI.

Italian Capuchins.   Odd fishes.

Lisbon, Sept. 9, 1760.

I Need not tell you that the crown of Portugal is possess'd of several ultramarine countries, the inhabitants of which are far from being all christians; and that all possible endeavours have been used for these two or three last centuries, to bring them all within the pale of the church, partly by most detestable acts of violence, as historians tell us, and partly by by the more lawful means of sending friars amongst them to preach them out of their ignorance and errors.

Amongst those friars, the capuchins have long enjoy'd the reputation of being the most zealous and most successful converters. But as their order was never established in this kingdom, the predecessors of his present Majesty thought fit to procure a number of them from those countries where they are established, and especially from France and Italy, where indeed there are enough to spare.

I suppose it was no very difficult matter for the first King of Portugal who thought of this scheme, to put it in execution, and to obtain from the Pope and their General the permission of importing as many capuchins here as were wanting. The design once formed, numbers of them came over in an uninterrupted succession; and as it was necessary for them all to learn this language before they were wafted over to their respective missions, they
were

were for a time, on their arrival here, scatter'd about the convents of the Franciscans, who are in reality little less than capuchins themselves, as the difference in their respective institutions chiefly consists in wearing a beard or no beard.

However, to lodge the Capuchins with people who shaved their chins, and somewhat jealous of their superior reputation for sanctity, was found productive of several inconveniencies. Therefore the late King came to the resolution of building two new convents in this capital, one for the French and the other for the Italian Capuchins, that each of the two bodies might live quite according to its own peculiar rules, depend on its own immediate superiors, and be by them directed to the acquisition of those means that would fit each friar for his speedy and distant peregrination.

On hearing of these two convents and their inhabitants I was presently kindled by the desire of seeing a number of my country-

countrymen collected together in one of them; and to satisfy that defire I fent *Batifte* yefterday to the *Father Guardian* of the Italians to beg of him, if it was not inconfiftent with their practices, as I fuppofed it was not, to give me a dinner any day he pleafed at their common table, together with the permiffion of fpending a whole afternoon in the company of his community.

My requeft was immediately granted, and the good *Guardian* pitch'd upon to-day, that I might be the fooner gratify'd. Accordingly this morning at ten o'clock, I went thither with the box of my chaife pretty well furnifhed with French bottles, as by way of return to their civility I thought of forcing them for once to fome extraordinary jollity by means of fuch liquors as I know they tafte but feldom.

The *Guardian* I found ready to receive me at the gate. He welcom'd me with infinite goodnefs, and feem'd perfectly

pleafed

pleased with so flattering a visit, as he termed it. In a moment I had the whole brotherhood about me, which consists of about fifteen or sixteen, all middle-aged, all healthy, and all very chearful. I must own that I was quite delighted to shake so many Italian hands, and to hear my native language uttered at once by so many mouths. They took me directly to the church where a *Pater* and *Ave* was soon said; then we visited the convent quite through, from the kitchen up to the library.

The convent stands upon an eminence on that end of the town which is furthest from the sea, and commands a prospect not much inferior to that of the Domicans of *Almada* on the opposite side of the river.

The habitations of the capuchins in Italy are in general narrow, poor, and unadorned: but this is quite otherwise, as the King who erected it, spared no expence to render it acceptable to the strangers

gers he invited over. Their church is a noble one, and richly ornamented, their dormitories and refectory are spacious and high-roofed, and their cells might as well be called very good rooms. The cieling of their library does not want stuccos, nor their shelves carvings; and the most precious *Brasil*-woods have been lavished in it as well as all about the convent.

As to the books in that library, there is not as yet the tenth part of what it might contain; and you may easily imagine that the greatest part of them are such, as can never pretend to the honour of admittance amongst those of the witty philosophers of the age. Some Latin Fathers simply bound make the first figure in the place: then many School-divines and Casuists, with a considerable number of Asceticks, and several collections of Italian and Portuguese sermons. Amongst which *Segueri* and *Vieyra* hold the first rank. A small shelf is filled up with manuscripts, chiefly catechisms and prayers

in

in several Indian and African languages, with some imperfect Grammars and Dictionaries, or rather Nomenclators of those same languages, compiled by former missionaries and deposited there for their successors to initiate themselves in them before they set out for those remote countries to which they are to go after a residence in Portugal of a few months.

Having spent full two hours in that library, the bell called us to the refectory. As we entered it, the friars placed themselves in two rows, one facing the other, and recited a long Latin grace with a sonorous tone of voice, those of one row answering alternately to those of the other with an edifying solemnity of devotion.

We now sat to a table that runs along the upper part of the place, and is made in the form of a greek Π. They placed me into the place of honour; that is, the middle point, the *Guardian* on my right, the *Vicar* on the left, and the rest on each side, except the youngest of them all,
who

who mounted a small pulpit and began to read a Latin compliment composed that very morning in commendation of some body present. That compliment I was obliged to swallow up to the last syllable, in spight of my several attempts to interrupt the perusal, and repeated intreaties that they would not make so prodigious a stranger of their own countryman. It was that arrant rogue *Batiste* who furnished the orator with his theme, as I immediately guess'd; and he was listening all the while at the door, heartily laughing at the discomposure and confusion of his old master; for which I gave him a good box on the ear while he was felicitating himself with old *Kelly* for his pretty contrivance on our return home.

Silence being dispensed by the *Guardian* out of favour to me, we all fell to our victuals with a brisk appetite, and though I had been very explicit in my message of yesterday about the treatment I expected, yet Father Cook thought

proper

proper for once to depart from his daily method, and gave us as many Italian and Portuguese ragoos as he could possibly manufacture. We were elevated to high mirth during the whole dinner. Jokes were crack'd by dozens, no matter whether witty or dull, and the bottles went round and round with as much briskness as if the *Guardian* and *Vicar* had been in Asia. They forced even a song out of me in a language of which none of them knew a single word. The banquet lasted an hour longer than it would have done if I had not been there, and ended with another Latin grace.

This great business being over, they took me to the garden, the circumference of which is near half a mile, perfectly well kept, and full of the choicest fruits. It lies on a sloping ground, and on the highest side of it there is a pretty large pond inhabited by a sort of fishes not to be found in any other place, as they believe. The creatures, as far as I could see, are about two spans long, and half as large, with a prominent bunch upon their backs, and not good to eat like other fishes. But what will surprize you to hear, they are of a nature so gay, that they prove quite astonishing. *Fishes, fishes,* cried the Guardian, *come to your dinner, come, come.* The fishes started up, sprang and tumbled about the water, seized the many pieces of bread that he threw to them, and then retired out of sight. The pleasantness of such a scene is not to be conceived. I begg'd that some of the company would preach them a sermon, hoping they would come out again and behave quite as well as those of the Adriatick upon a certain occasion. The Fathers took the joke, and smiled, and wondered I had not forgot my pretty Italian stories in my long absence from my native country.

We then play'd at bowls under the grape-bowers, and, above all, chatted incessantly. But what took my fancy most, was a translation of one of the Cantos

Cantos of the *Jerusalem delivered* in the *Genoese* dialect which one of the Fathers read to the company. This, he said, was a juvenile composition of his; and I thought it excellent in its kind. They are all subjects of the republic of *Genoa*, and have been successively so for many years, as a medley of them, formed at first out of the several Italian states, was judged inconvenient soon after their introduction in Portugal.

Towards evening I took my leave with a million of thanks for their kindness and good treatment; went to the coffee-house, as usual; then came home and scribbled thus far: and now I have nothing further to tell, but that to-morrow I will begin a journey to *Mafra*, *Cintra*, and some other places.

LETTER XXVII.

A short excursion. Sad accommodations. Thanks to Aurora.

Cintra, Sept. 11, 1760.

THOSE who have never gone twenty miles from home, are apt to fancy that travelling is a very pretty thing. But let him who holds this opinion, come to travel about Portugal, and I will submit to eat thistles if he does not stagger in his notions about travelling.

I have now been two days out of *Lisbon*, because I suffered myself to be seduced by the desire of seeing *Mafra* and *Cintra*. But I pay dear for my folly, as I have undergone more misery during these two days than ever fell to the share of any man during two centuries. The expression sounds odd: but you know that extreme pain makes people mad.

The

The deplorable account of thefe two days hardfhips and torments is now conveyed to you by means of this letter from a room on the ground-floor of a houfe half-ruined, that goes in this country under the appellation of an' inn, and would be thought in any other a rendezvous for witches.

The furniture of this room confifts of three things. An ill-hewn bit of a fir-plank, which by means of three crooked fticks has obtained the name of ftool; a tottering old table as fmooth as a rafp; and a piece of coarfe and dirty canvafs ftretch'd wide upon the dufty floor made of broken bricks: and this is the beft bed that this inn could afford. Ye unfortunate bones that crack'd fo many times laft night upon the ftony couch at *Mafra!* how fhall I fave you from breaking by and by when extended upon thefe uneven bricks, where I muft lay myfelf for wearinefs!

But

But let me begin the sad chronicle from yesterday morning and bring it orderly down to this woeful evening: and while I take a pinch of snuff to quicken my narration, take yourselves a cordial that your hearts may not fail you while you read it.

Yesterday morning therefore, a little before seven, I got into my chaise, attended by old *Kelly* on horseback, and sat out for *Mafra:* but my brown mules went along with so senatorial a pace, that it was past twelve when we reached a village called *Cabeza,* about twelve miles distant from *Lisbon.*

At the inn of *Cabeza* we stopped with a mind to get a dinner, if there was any to be got. A smiling little fellow showed me to a room, which would be a tolerable lodging for a *Gypsey* or a *Jew*, was it not that it admits too much light through the chinks of the cieling or roof, and that the floor is

not

not near so well paved as the great road.

It presently occurr'd that the smiling little fellow had mistaken *Kelly* and me for the mules, and the mules for us: therefore I stepp'd to see how they were accommodated; and indeed I found that they had been received in an apartment much larger and cleaner than ours: however I did not think proper to change places, because, if our room had a perforated roof, theirs had no roof at all.

We should have had neither dinner that could be eaten, nor wine that could be drank, if *Kelly* had not desired his wife at all events to put something better than straw in the box of the chaise; and the good woman had dropp'd into it a pigeon-pye, a roasted turkey, and a Barbary-tongue, together with half a dozen bottles of the best wine. By means of such provender we baffled the design of the *Cabeza* host, who wanted to poison us with stinking lard and with a fowl that my negro found quite as tender as the tail of an old alligator. The smiling rogue! Beware of fellows that smile for ever!

At night we reached *Mafra*, about eight miles distant from *Cabeza*. The whole country from *Lisbon* to *Mafra* (very few spots excepted) may very well dispute the praise of sterility with any desart in *Nubia*.

The supper that was offered us there, was not a bit inferior to the dinner at *Cabeza*. But our turkey had yet lost no more than a wing and a leg, and of the pigeon-pye two good thirds were still in store.

But when the hour came to go to bed, what eloquence could ever express the misery I was to undergo! I was led into a room, whose cieling was open from space to space. In that room there was a bed which, though not quite so wide as *America*, had still several wild nations
scat-

scattered all about, all painted black, and all as nimble as any Indians.

I will leave it for you to guess whether I could shut my eyes a moment during the whole night amidst so many enemies! Lucid Aurora! I humbly thank thee for thy early coming to call me out of that bed. Whatever flesh and blood I have still left, I will henceforwards acknowledge as thy gift; and thy gift likewise was that appetite which permitted me to eat half a melon for my breakfast.

After breakfast I paid my visit to the Royal Convent, the description of which you shall have to-morrow, if ever I get up alive from this piece of canvas, on which I am going to lay myself through mere impossibility of keeping my body in a sitting posture.

LETTER XXVIII.

Promontorium Lunæ. Holes, and Holes, and Holes again. An odd evening walk. A chearful dinner. Coins dropp'd to a Mary Magdalen for a very good reason.

Cintra, Sept. 12, 1760.

I Have had the good luck to secure such a bed for to-night, and passed the day besides with so perfect a satisfaction, that the dirty canvas and uneven bricks are already forgotten. And so goes this fickle world! A perpetual shifting from good to evil, and from evil to good.

And now the natural order of things seems to require a description of the Royal Convent: but what I have seen to-day presses a great deal more upon my fancy, and my impatience of imparting to you a share of the pleasure I have received myself to-day, makes me invert the laws of narration without any great hesitation.

This

This morning early I quitted this place along with my trusty *Kelly*. Leaving the mules and the horse at the inn, each of us got astride upon a jack-ass; and so we went up a high and steep mountain to see a convent of *Jeronimites* which is on the summit of it.

That convent could formerly contain near a dozen of inhabitants; yet at present there are but four or five, because a part of it has been demolished by the earthquake. What is left of it consists of five or six rooms supported by a portico that encloses a court-yard. This yard is paved chequer-wise with white and blue tiles of earthen ware, and so disposed as to collect all the rain-water into a cistern under it. The walls of the portico are likewise incrusted with such parti-colour'd tiles.

From the windows an extensive prospect is commanded, as that summit is near a mile higher than the level of the sea. The eye runs freely over an immense tract

tract of country, too much of it quite barren.

The middle parts of the hill seem composed of numberless broken rocks, some as big as houses. Yet between rock and rock the Fathers have cultivated several small bits of ground, which furnish their little community with more pulse and herbage than they want. It is pity that no fruit-tree will grow there, because of the sharp air and chilling mists: so that whatever fruit they have, is fetched every day from *Cintra* with their other provisions, and carried up to them upon asses of their own. But besides herbs and pulse they cultivate Turkey-corn, with which they make savoury cakes for themselves and visitors, and feed poultry with the overplus.

To the summit of that mountain there is no access but by the path we went. Every other side consists of cliffs upon cliffs, inaccessible even to goats.

As

As the church and the convent were originally built in a moſt ſolid manner, the earthquake had not ſtrength enough to demoliſh them intirely, though it was felt as violent there as in any other part of Portugal: nor did any of the friars periſh, though the whole mountain was horribly ſhaken. The church ſtands on the very ſpot that was formerly occupied by a Roman temple dedicated to the Moon, which had given the name of *Promontorium Lunæ* to the hill. This ſcrap of erudition I got from one of the friars.

We ſtay'd there about two hours; then came down afoot, our jack-aſſes driven before us by the Negro. About mid-mountain I hired a guide to ſhow us the way to another hill near two leagues from this. The fellow took us about and about through a pathleſs country, partly covered with looſe pieces of rocks, partly heathy, and partly ſandy. Yet from ſpace to ſpace we met with numbers of

ſir

fir and cork-trees, with some small oaks and a few other plants, that contribute to render several parts of it romantically beautiful.

The place we were going to, stands on the summit of another mountain no less high than the supposed *Promontorium Lunæ*, called by the Portuguese *Cabo de Roca*, and by the English *the Rock of Lisbon*. I hope you have not forgot that Rock, and the pleasure it gave me when I saw it for the first time. It was the *Cork-Convent* on its summit I wanted to visit, and we reached it with some difficulty, as we went to it by a cross-road extremely rugged and steep, and over several precipices that demanded much attention both from us and from our asses.

The *Cork-Convent* is properly a hermitage; and you have but one path to it under a kind of arch irregularly cut through a piece of rock by the hand of nature. That arch is about two hundred
steps

steps below the hermitage, and all other parts near that summit are perfectly pathless and not to be clamber'd.

Near that arch we left our asses in the custody of our guide, and ascended the rest of the mountain a-foot. And here, ye Muses nine, I invoke your assistance! Help me to an adequate description of the oddest, wildest, most romantic, and most pleasing place that ever I was in!

The hermits had discover'd us from a-far; therefore we found them ready to receive us. We bow'd, shook hands, and seem'd as pleased as if we had long been most intimate friends. The Father Superiour ask'd us whether we had dined, and being answer'd in the negative, dispatched one of his Friars to make something ready as fast as possible. He then took us to see the place which begins with a flat irregular area about forty yards square.

The area is fronted by a huge rock variously perforated; and its various perforaforations, caverns, or holes form the hermitage. The church of it is a hole; the facrifty a hole; the confeffion-room a hole; the kitchin a hole; the dormitory a hole; the refectory a hole; every cell a hole; and the doors and windows of all thefe holes are ftill nothing elfe but fo many other holes. But fo narrow are thofe which form the doors of the cells, that fhould a man grow hydropic while in one of them, he never would be able to come out of it; and the cells themfelves are fo fmall, that no tall friar when in his bed has room enough to extend his legs. Yet in them they lie at night upon ftraw-bags, after having taken the precaution to fhut what they call their doors and windows with fmall planks.

Not one hole in the whole place deferves the epithet of fpacious. The largeft is that which they term *the Kitchen*. A French cook would be angry at the proftitution of fo noble a word, but the friars are not fo fcrupulous. The fmoke

of

of that kitchen is carried out by a cylindrical perforation over the fire-place.

Dame Nature indeed was in a merry mood when she took it into her fancy to form so whimsical a place. You cannot conceive what little help she received from art to fit it for its present inhabitants. The earthquake shook it to and fro, and, they say, with inconceivable violence. Yet that violence proved vain, and I do not wonder at it. The demolition of the hermitage cannot be effected but by the fall of the mountain.

What adds to the singularity of this natural edifice is, that every part in it is covered with cork; the walls, floors, and all. And this is the reason why the English sailors call it *the Cork-Convent*. That cork prevents the bad effects of the dampness which would otherwise be very inconvenient, as many parts of its walls are cover'd with a thin moss, and the water distils through the pores of the rock in very small drops.

From the hermitage they descend by a range of irregular steps to a piece of water and to their several spots of garden. Not far from that water there is another hole, in which one of their predecessors had the patience to live the last twenty years of his life, without ever quitting it day or night. At least you are told so by an inscription over that hole, absurdly supported by the testimony of the friars themselves, who were all born near two centuries after, according to the inscription, which I wish fairly destroy'd and the hole filled up for their own sake, as the place has no need of a lye to induce people to visit it. No human being could ever live in that hole for several reasons that I will forbear to tell.

I said that there is a piece of water on that eminence, which fertilizes several spots. The friars are all gardeners and have vegetables of various sorts in great abundance, but no fruit. The many
steps

steps by which they descend to that water, they term humourously their *evening walk*; and, abating the inconvenience of the steps, it is really a pleasant walk, shaded with many trees and bushes.

After having visited the whole hermitage we went to dinner. In the midst of that hole that is called the Refectory, a stone serves them for a table whenever the rain forces them to eat their victuals under shelter. But to-day, as the weather was very fine, we chose to dine in the area. Being a meagre day we had an ample dish of salt-fish most savourily dress'd after the manner of the country with garlick and *pimenta*, a large sallad, and Dutch cheese with pears, apples, grapes, and figs, ten times more than we could eat, good bread, and excellent wine. During dinner the hermits kept us in chat with the greatest good humour; told us of the many English gentlemen and ladies that visit them, and help'd us to our glasses very briskly. The wine was good, and we could not help drinking the English Ladies.

These hermits are of the Franciscan order; therefore will touch no money: but there is a *Mary Magdalen* painted over a kind of altar in the church; and to Mary Magdalen you drop a coin slily. It would not otherwise be in the power of this little community to furnish their numerous visitors with meat and drink, and entertain besides a good number of poor people who visit the place, partly out of devotion and partly to get a meal. They admit ladies to visit the hermitage when they are in company with gentlemen; otherwise not: and as to women of low rank, they are not allowed to ascend beyond the Arch mentioned before, except on some festival days.

About an hour after dinner we took our leave and went back to our asses who had leisurely cropp'd the thistles about, while our guide and the Negro feasted merrily upon herrings, cheese, and fruit,

con-

convey'd to them with a sufficient quantity of bread and wine by one of the fathers.

And now I may truly say that I have seen the strangest solitude that ever was inhabited by men, amidst the most pleasing assemblage of craggs, rocks, trees, and bushes that can possibly be fancied; the whole commanding a most wide and amazing prospect, as from thence you discover a vast tract of the ocean with many of the castles and habitations at the mouth of the *Tagus,* the tops of the Royal Convent of *Mafra,* several villages and hamlets, with many single cottages scatter'd over a long chain of uneven mountains, some of which are perfectly rocky and barren; some shaded with oaks, fir-trees, and cork-trees; and some cover'd with vines, olive-trees, and lemon or orange-groves, besides numberless other plants of every kind and generation.

LETTER XXIX.

Vaſt many teeth a-going in a great houſe. Genealogical books. The excellence of the circular figure. Gallantry of a devout King.

Liſbon, Sept. 13, 1760, in the forenoon.

I Am here again ready to give you an account of *Mafra* and *Cintra*.

Mafra is so inconſiderable a village, that the name of it would not be found in a map of *Portugal*, were it not for a vaſt pile which King *John* V., Father to his preſent Majeſty, cauſed to be erected within a muſket-ſhot of it.

That pile, which is perfectly quadrangular, conſiſts of a church, two royal apartments, and a convent. The church and apartments take up one half of it, and the convent the other half.

The church is placed in the middle of the chief front towards the village, and is ſpacious enough to contain more than a thousand people, exclusive of the choir: but it is so very dark, that you cannot see at one glance all the fine things in it; which is to be regretted, as neither gold, nor silver, bronze, precious marbles, nor even the dearest jewels, have been spared to render it an object of astonishment.

There are several altars in it, each as rich as art and money could make it. The chief one has a statue of massy silver, with several large candlesticks, and so many other rich ornaments, that it cost (they say) half a million of crusadoes (a), and I am inclined to credit the assertion.

There are likewise six organs, three on each side, but none of them as yet finished. When they are, it will be curious to hear them all play in concert. People hope that the effect will prove extremely pleasing, but I am not quite sure of it, and am afraid of confusion. The church,

(a). *A Crusado is something more than an English half-crown.*

as I apprehend, is not ample enough for a collection of so much sound. However I may be mistaken.

Of the two royal apartments, that on the right side of the church as you go in, is called *the Queen's,* and that on the left *the King's.* Both are large enough to afford a commodious lodgement to their Majesties and their attendants. Each is formed by a long range of rooms, closets, and halls, and each communicates with the other by means of a passage over a part of the church. I don't know how they are furnished, because the furniture is always laid up whenever their Majesties leave the place. The two principal staircases which lead up to the apartments, are well lighted, sufficiently wide, and perfectly easy.

Each corner of that chief front supports a dome somewhat in the form of a pavillion. Those domes viewed at a proper distance have a fine effect, and con-

trast

trast surprisingly well with the cupola, and the four belfrys in the church.

The whole of that chief front is really as noble as art could possibly make it. The gate in the middle of it has on each side an insulated column of a kind of granite found somewhere in this country which is little inferior to the Egyptian. Each column was cut out of a single block, and each is about three fathoms in circumference.

On each side of that gate there is a portico supported by other fine columns, and ornamented with several gigantic statues made at Rome by excellent masters. However the porticos seemed to me rather too small for those statues, or the statues too big for the porticos.

But what struck me most on that side of the edifice, is the ascent to the church. That ascent takes up the best part of the space between the edifice and the village, and the wide semicircular steps of it make

it

it appear so very grand, that I question whether we have in Italy any thing of the kind that can be compared to it.

The roof of the apartments and the church, exclusive of the pavillion, the cupola, and the belfrys, is laid out in a kind of terrace that commands an extensive prospect. The belfrys contain a hundred and sixty bells of various sizes, and upon them many curious chimes are rung by means of some engines which are contained in two towers beneath. But it is impossible to give an idea of those engines without a number of drawings. It is enough to tell you, that they have cost near a million of crusadoes. They are in fact the greatest object of curiosity in the whole place, and the art of clock-making was, I think, quite exhausted in those two towers. So many wheels! So many springs, pivots, rods, some of brass and some of steel! Who would attempt a description? A vast deal of thinking has been lavish'd there: yet both the money and

and the ingenuity has all been fquander'd to produce nothing elfe but fome bell-mufic, which muft prove difguftful if it lafts more than three minutes.

There are, amongft many fine parts, two court-yards there, that are furrounded by the fineft porticos I ever faw; finer than the *Procuratie Nove* at Venice. The porticos fupport feveral apartments for the officers of ftate when the court is there. Thofe apartments as well as thofe of their Majefties, communicate with that part of the building that has been allowed to the friars.

That part confifts of three dormitories, a refectory, an infirmary, a kitchen, a library, and fome other places.

One of the three dormitories I take to be about three hundred common fteps in length, and wide enough for ten men to walk a-breaft. They fay that the cells on each fide of the three dormitories are above fix hundred: nor are they narrow and low as in all other Francifcan convents,

vents, but fpacious and high vaulted; fo that each might as well be termed a room fit for any Roman prelate to live in. However the mafs-friars there, are not fo numerous as the cells. They are but three hundred, and the lay-friars a hundred and fifty.

The furniture of each cell (thofe of the mafs-friars I mean) confifts of a narrow uncover'd bed, (not very foft) a table, a few chairs, a fhelf for books, and very little elfe. The lay-friars have no fhelves, as the beft part of them cannot read.

As to the refectory, it is a glorious thing. The table that runs through it, admits of more than a hundred and fifty people on each fide. By this you may judge of its length: yet there is room enough left at one end of it for another table, at which the King will fometimes dine with fome of his grandees.

As I entered the refectory a little before the friars went to dinner, the cloth was laid; and I could not help taking notice, that

that for every two they have a mug which contains about two bottles of wine. Thofe mugs are all alike, of white earthen-ware, with the arms of the King on each. Befides the mugs, there are trenchers of *Brafil*-wood, one for every two friars, with fix figs upon it, two bunches of grapes, and two lemons. The reft of their dinner (I have not feen it) confifts of three good difhes, fat or meagre as the day happens to be. Each friar has a wheaten loaf that weighs about a pound. Should they want more, they afk for more.

When the three hundred *Padres* are at dinner, the hundred and fifty lay-friars wait behind with the greateft refpect. It is the King that furnifhes them with that food which makes them all look fo florid and jolly. Such faces I never faw in my life, not even in the pictures of *Paul Veronefe*, who delighted in painting friars handfome.

They

They say that the maintenance of this great family costs the King no less than two hundred thousand crusadoes a year: nor do I think it an exaggeration, considering that at the rate of thirty two good teeth for each mouth, there are above fourteen thousand teeth a-going twice a day the whole year round. Then there is the additional expence of their morning-chocolate, their cloaths, their firing, their great consumption of wax in the church and in the cells; the candles and lamps in their dormitories and kitchen, besides many other articles tedious to enumerate. What costs but little, is their infirmary; but it must be observ'd that when any of them begins to grow old or turns sickly, he is sent to some other convent, and one young and healthy substituted in his room. Their infirmary I have not seen, nor their kitchen.

Their library takes up a very large hall, besides a pretty large room. The hall
contains

contains little less than seventy thousand volumes, and the room about ten thousand, as I was told. Amongst these last there are as many Portuguese books as could possibly be collected. I looked over the labels of a long quarto-shelf on the right hand as you go in, and saw that they were all genealogical. If the authors of those quartos have adhered to truth, no nation under the sun is so well apprised of their ancestors as this. There is scarce a family of any note throughout the kingdom but what can boast of an historian, and many have had more than one. Hence (foreigners say) that noble elevation of mind which makes the Portuguese look with the greatest disdain upon all other nations and despise every thing that is not Portuguese: and hence perhaps (I say myself) the source of that immense rage which invaded the whole soul of the Duke *D'Aveiro*, and induced him to commit one of those actions, which never failed to bring ruin upon

their

their perpetrators, as the hiſtories of all times and nations will tell us. That Duke could not bear with patience to have a few pages of his genealogical book blotted by any body.

Beſides that vaſt number of genealogies in quarto and other ſizes, there are in that leſſer library many hiſtories of the Portugueſe conqueſts in various parts of the ultramarine world. Then follow the theological and devotional books, which are far from being few. This to me is a proof that the Portugueſe are pious and ſkilful in divinity. But what abounds there without meaſure, are the lives of Saints, male and female, foreign and domeſtic. They ſay that St. Anthony alone has above a hundred volumes on thoſe ſhelves, each telling his atchievements in a different manner. No Alexander, no Auguſtus, no King of Pruſſia ever was honoured with ſo much biography as good St. Anthony.

According

According to the Father Librarian, that leſſer library is much more valuable than the greater. And in one reſpect he is certainly right. The books in the greater may be procured for love or money: but not thoſe in the leſſer, becauſe Portugueſe books are become very ſcarce ever ſince the earthquake. The fire that follow'd it, has deſtroyed many public and private libraries in this metropolis, and a Portugueſe book of any note is now become as dear as a ruby.

However the loſs of Portugueſe learning will ſcarcely be felt out of Portugal, as it never was in faſhion any where, and will ſcarcely ever be. Few are the writers of this country who ever had a name abroad. *Oſorio* the Latin hiſtorian is certainly a name much conſidered in the literary world, and that of *Camoens*, the Portugueſe Epic, has travelled beyond *Allentejo* and *Eſtremadura*. Yet the works of theſe two are more commended than read. Our Italian friars extol one of their sacred orators called *Vieira*, and put him upon a par with our *Segneri*: But I have not the greatest opinion of our friars' taste in point of oratory. I have opened one of *Vieira*'s volumes in that library, and chance directed my eyes upon the proem of a sermon, in which the perfections of the circular figure are pompously enumerated; after which the *Lusitanian Cicero* (as his countrymen call him) proceeds to tell his audience, that *if the Supreme Being was to show himself under any geometrical figure, that would certainly be the circular in preference to the triangular, the square, the pentagonal, the duodecagonal, or any other known to the geometricians.* What could I do after having read such a proem, but hastily replace the book on the shelf? However *Vieira*'s works must have power, as they are much esteemed by a great number of people, and I wish I had time to spare, to see in what that power consists.

Before

Before I went to *Mafra* I had heard of a Portuguese version of *Metastasio*'s Operas, and asked of the Father Librarian to show it me. But he had it not, nor had as yet heard of it. And what do you think that version is? I am assured that the translator has given the Metastasian heroes many livery-servants, who take possession of the scene as fast as their respective masters go off, and have dialogues of their own with the chambermaids and nurses of the heroines. You laugh! But what fault can you find in *Achilles* having a running footman, *Semiramis* a dry-nurse, or *Deidamia* a little prating hussey of a cook-maid who bids the negro-boy to carry the chocolate up to his mistress? If this is the dramatic taste in Portugal, a version of *Goldoni*'s works would make the Portuguese full as happy, as the text does the Venetian gondoliers.

The Portuguese have a dictionary of their own language which is much commended both by themselves and by foreigners.

reigners. But it was not the work of a native. Father *Bluteau*, a French Jesuit, compiled it. It is printed in eight or nine large quarto volumes. I wanted to buy it, but so many volumes are too cumbersome for a traveller; besides that the earthquake has put the price of it almost out of the reach of my purse.

I skimm'd over several other Portuguese books in the space of four hours that I passed in that library. In a medical one I read of a remedy for sore eyes, which seems no less excellent than singular. *The person thus afflicted*, says the Portuguese physician, *must neither read nor look on any white wall*. The good-natured Librarian was in raptures to see me so inquisitive about the learning of his country: but if I am allowed to draw inferences from the little I pick'd up there, the most famed Portuguese writers are at best but equal to our *Achillini's* and *Ciampoli's* in verse, and to our *Giuglari's* and *Tesauro's* in prose, whose distorted way

way of thinking and turgidness of expression have procured the appellation of *Secolo cattivo* to the last century, whenever we consider it in a literary light. Our tumid *Calloandro's*, *Eromena's*, *Dianea's*, *Coralbo's*, and other books of that kind, seem translations from the Portuguese. However, I wish again I had leisure to look for a few months into the learning of this country.

The large library at *Mafra*, I had no time to examine. Yet I have seen enough of it to know that it is a very good one. Besides the best books in the learned languages, I am told that it contains some valuable manuscripts, particulary in Hebrew and in Arabic; and as I have seen several of the friars studying there, it is most probable that some of them are learned. But a traveller had need to stay a considerable time in such places, in order to come away with just ideas of the people, and this unluckily was not in my power at *Mafra*.

Let me now take my leave of the Father Librarian and enter the garden of the convent. It is pretty ample, confidering that it has been in a manner cut out of the folid rock, and much of the earth in it tranfported from diftant places. It has a large refervoir in the middle, befides feveral fountains. From fome doors in the walls of it, you may enter the royal park, enclofed likewife by a wall, which, they fay, is fourteen or fifteen miles round. The little I faw of that park from the windows of the cells, far from being embellifhed by that verdure which fmiles the whole year round in the parks of England, has very much the appearance of a parch'd and rocky defart thinly fcattered with trees.

But it is the building that deferves all one's attention. Few edifices in Europe (perhaps not ten) ftand fo majeftick upon the face of the globe. The original architect was a German who had been bred at Rome; and a very dilated genius he

muft

muſt have had to imagine ſo vaſt a fabrick and adjuſt all the parts of it in ſo noble and convenient a manner as he has done. The firſt ſtone of it was laid in 1717, if I am rightly informed; and yet ſome of its internal parts are not quite finiſhed, though more than ſix thouſand workmen were conſtantly employed upon it during the firſt twenty years, beſides numberleſs artiſts in Rome and other parts.———
It is but lately that the number of thoſe workmen has been conſiderably diminiſhed. At preſent there are but two hundred.

The occaſion of the building of it, was a vow made by the archdutcheſs who married King John V. On her approaching the coaſt of Portugal the firſt land ſhe ſpy'd was the hills of *Mafra*, and the firſt favour ſhe aſked of her royal ſpouſe was, that he would erect a temple there to the Virgin Mary and St. Anthony, to whoſe joint protection ſhe owned herſelf indebted for her ſafe landing in Portugal.

tugal. His Majesty, the most friar-ridden King that ever existed, easily granted her request. He went even so far beyond it, as to add the palace, the convent, the garden, and the park, that he might duely honour the whole spot that was bless'd by the first glance of his august Bride. An odd piece of gallantry! As there are immense quarries of beautiful marbles and hard stones all over the neighbourhood of *Mafra*, the good Queen had the satisfaction before she died to see the edifice far advanced and decorated with more than fifty gigantick statues.

LETTER XXX.

No learning in a second life. Ignorance of knowing men. Organs and clock-work. Moorish ornaments.

Lisbon, Sept. 13, 1760. *in the Evening.*

AFTER having leisurely visited the royal convent, I was taken back to the church by the King's organ-maker,

maker, who wanted to show me the internal parts of one of the six organs.

Those parts I have examined with the greatest attention, and the use of each I have heard most minutely explained. But my ignorance of the organ-making-art is such, that I dare not venture upon the least sketch of a description. How negligent have I been not to have bestow'd a single thought in the space of forty years upon tubes and bellows, that I might easily conceive how a vast variety of enchanting sounds is drawn from them! But too many are the things that a man ought to have studied to be properly qualified for a writer of travels.

Most people, when they consider the opportunities they have neglected of enlarging knowledge which it was a thousand times in their power to enlarge, have got a conceit that, were they to begin life a-new, they would apply with the keenest eagerness and most stubborn resolution to all sciences, and fill up their

minds

minds with whatever was known in this world ever since the days of *Pythagoras* and *Aristotle*.

But such speculatists have no right notions of things, in my opinion. Let our lives be ever so protracted, and our application ever so unremitted, I think it is providential that we are not early sensible of the much that there is for us to learn, and of the little that we can learn. Was this not the case, we would be scared away from the approaches of knowledge, and, instead of acquiring the little which we do, it is my firm opinion that we would never have courage to set about acquiring any.

Indeed it is lucky that we begin our voyage through the ocean of learning quite unconscious of its immensity, otherwise our poor hearts would fail us at once, and we would do like the lazy wench, who having the house to clean, the beds to make, the dishes to wash, and the dinner to dress, grew so desperate,

rate, that she ran up to the garret, threw herself on her bed, and fell asleep.

Such is the train of ideas that my ignorance about organ-making has produced. What a contempt must that artist have conceived of me, on his finding me so little instructed in so noble a science! Yet I have this comfort, that his contempt would have reached many a greater man, as many there are, who, like myself, are quite ignorant of things much below that of organ-making. How various are the scholars in the various universities of Europe who eat bread twice or thrice a-day, and yet are utter strangers to the art of baking? How many those, who are perpetually dipping their quills in a standish, and yet know not how common ink is made? How many who are shaved every morning, and never thought to enquire about the ingredients that compose soap?

I recollect a story to this purpose which seems to me worth relating. Three English

lish wits, *Walsh*, *Wycherley*, and *Pope*, walking together along the side of a field, were once engaged in a dispute about a blade of grass which one of them chanced to pick up. This is a most beautiful blade of *wheat*, said one of them; I never saw a finer! It is no wheat at all, said the other; I take it to be *rye*. Fy upon you both, interrupted the third, it is neither rye nor wheat, but it is *oats* as sure as I am alive. *Miller* the Botanist happen'd to go by as they began to look cross upon each other. They ask'd him; and so it happen'd that none of the three was right.

The greatest part of what we call men of learning, are ignorant of the most common things, and philosophers might learn from the very lowest of the people more than some of them imagine: I must therefore not fret because an organ-maker has taken me for a blockhead. He was right so far as he went.

The name of this man is *Eugene Nicholas Egan*, a native of Ireland. He is scarce four foot high; but what body he has is all alive. He has obtained his place at *Mafra* neither by chance nor protection, but by dint of skill. The King had caused eight famous organ-makers to come to Portugal from Italy, Germany, and other parts; and he whose organ should prove best, was to have that place. You may well imagine that each strove to conquer his rivals. But the immortal Castrato *Caffarello*, together with the celebrated composer *David Perez*, having been deputed to judge of their several performances, unanimously decided in favour of little *Egan*'s, and of course he had the place. His salary proved afterwards not so ample as he expected: but what is a salary to a genius? He has defeated his enemies; he has seen them quit Portugal with shame.

After having shewn me his organ, play'd a good while upon it, and repeatedly

edly touched a treble which is an invention of his own, he took me to see the best friend he has in *Mafra*, the man who rings the bells of the royal convent.

You are not to laugh when I tell you that I had the honour to pay a visit to His Majesty's bell-ringer, who is as great a man as ever pulled the ropes of a bell, and as eminent in his way as *Plato* was in his own. Besides that he can make those bells sound in regular subordination, he can also ring so many curious chimes upon them, that he delights the whole court. But what constitutes him a great man and a genius, are two instruments he has invented, one form'd of many bits of wood, the other of many bits of brick. Those bits he lays down in a particular order upon a table: then takes up two small wooden hammers, and plays upon them. What sweetness is contained in wood and bricks! Upon both he plays the very best overtures of *Handel* and the most difficult lessons of

Scar-

Scarlatti. Master *Egan*, who has himself added a new treble to the Organ, and of course is a proper judge of these matters, honours and loves this man, though but a Bell-ringer, and is not jealous of his abilities because they do not interfere with his own.

The sun was going down apace when I took my leave of those two wonderful men. I shook hands with the bell-ringer and could not help embracing the pretty dwarf.

The road between *Mafra* and *Cintra* is still such as it was after the flood when the waters subsided, and I alighted twenty times from my chaise for fear of being overturned. I saw on both sides the road in many places many stone-blocks and marble-columns, as the quarries are there that have furnished the materials for the Royal Convent. It was dark when I reached *Cintra*, and my Negro took me to *the English Inn*; so called because it is chiefly kept up by a society of

English

English merchants, who go thither from *Lisbon*, either upon pleasure or to buy up oranges and lemons. When those merchants are there, they get the best rooms, and with a very good reason, as they have fitted it themselves for their own reception.

It happen'd that the whole house was full on my arrival, and as it was too late to procure any lodging, I was obliged to sleep upon the mentioned piece of canvas in a neighbouring house. But on my return from the *Cork-convent* the merchants were gone, and I had an excellent bed.

It is now time to tell you, that, before the earthquake, *Cintra* was very well worth a visit. A royal palace was there which is now almost destroy'd. They say that it was many centuries ago one of the country-seats of the *Moorish* Kings that wrested *Portugal* and *Spain* from the hands of the *Vandals*, who had themselves wrested both countries from those of the *Romans*.

Romans. *Moorish* or not *Moorish*, I see by its ruins, as well as by what remains standing, that it was once a great palace. There are still three of its halls to be seen. The ceiling of each is divided into little spaces that have animals painted in them. But each ceiling had but one animal allotted towards its ornament; and thus one contains nothing else but so many *swans*, the other nothing else but *stags*, and the third nothing else but *magpyes*. An odd taste of decoration, especially as the swans, the stags, and magpyes are uniform, and the posture of each the same as that of the next. Each swan has a golden chain round his neck; each stag supports a coat of arms on his back; and each magpye has the words *per ben* written by her side; which words, preceded by that of *Piga*, form an allusive *Moorish* quibble I have already forgot.

The walls of the three halls are incrustated with square pieces of marble of two different colours disposed chequerwise, wife, and so are the floors. On the ground-floor there is a small room where before the earthquake water was made to spout from many little pipes concealed in the walls on the touching of a spring; and this is almost all that is left of that *Moorish* palace. They are rebuilding it, and the King will have it restored to its ancient form. A laudable thought, as posterity will still see what was the *Moorish* taste in architecture.

From the windows of the hall where the stags are painted, there is a fine prospect; but I am sick of prospects, and will give you no further description of any. If you love prospects, get upon steeples.

The royal convent at *Mafra* has not suffer'd much by the earthquake. The friars made me observe, that the little round members over the plinths of the two great columns on each side the gate of the church, were crack'd and partly broken off. But that was almost all the damage

damage the building has undergone, though the trepidation of the ground was fo great, that fome of the friars were thrown upon their faces as they were kneeling in the choir, and many people in the church ftumbled againſt each other. Had the building inclined but an inch or two more, it would probably have gone down all at once and crufh'd them all in an inftant.

I take now my leave of *Cintra*; of the beautiful fpot it ftands upon, of the remaining halls of the *Moorifh* palace, and of the high hills in that neighbourhood, where many Englifh and many Portuguefe have pretty country-houfes. I am told that not far from thence there is a fpot of ground about a league in length and a mile broad, all planted with oranges and lemons, whofe flowers in due feafon perfume a vaft tract of country. They call it the valley of *Collares*, and compare it to the garden of *Eden*. In all probability, had I gone to fee it, I

fhould

should have compared it to the territory of *San Remo* on the Ligurian coast.

As I came from *Cintra* towards Lisbon I saw some other parts of that Aqueduct that goes over the valley of *Alcantara*. I saw likewise some agreeable *Quintas*; that is, *Country-houses* belonging to the Portuguese nobility and gentry. Yet in general the country which I have seen during this short ramble, is rocky and barren.

LETTER XXXI.

People forbidden to talk. Robbers and not Murtherers. Concussion from east to west. Barraca's. Blacks and their progenies. Jews and their perverseness. Creaking of wheels.

Lisbon, Sept. 15. 1760.

MY enquiries here have not merely been limited to customs and manners, to palaces and convents. I have done my utmost to collect genuine information

formation about the several transactions which have lately turned the eyes of all Europe to this country, and you would admire my industry if I were to apprise you of all my endeavours to find the true motive of the Duke *D'Aveiro*'s crime, the expulsion of the Jesuits, the banishment of the King's natural brothers, the unprecedented harsh treatment to Cardinal *Acciajoli*, and the exaltation of Don Bastian Joseph *de Carvalho* to the very summit of power.

These subjects are certainly worth inquiry, especially as care has been taken to throw a veil over them, which will obstruct future historians. But my diligence of search has not been much rewarded. This government has forbidden every body to make these, and other current matters, the topics of their conversation: the prohibition subjects the transgressors to such severe penalties, and so many have already been thrown into jail upon this account, that the poor souls are quite frighted at the mere mention of some names: nor is it easy to bring any native to disclose his opinion about any thing that looks political, though forwardness to decide and love of talking are two of the chief ingredients in the character of the Portuguese. As for the few particularities which I have been able to glean from foreigners, they are so full of uncertainty, contradiction, and evident partiality, that instead of making them any part of my letters, it will be better to save them for oral entertainment.

But I cannot quit this country without saying a few words more of the Jesuits. From a brother who writes from *Portugal*, you have a kind of right to expect his opinion of them, as well as of the proceedings of this government against them.

As you are well acquainted with my way of thinking on several particulars, you will possibly imagine that I approve
of

of thofe proceedings, and that I confider thefe pretended *Companions of Jefus* as a gang of traitors always ready to ftab Sovereigns and overthrow kingdoms, as they are confidered by numberlefs people throughout Europe. But, whatever be the opinion of others, I never could do them fo much honour as to think them poffeffed of that fteadinefs of foul which is required to venture upon fuch great and bold acts of wickednefs. I have often watched them as an Order, and have likewife been intimately acquainted with a good number of their individuals; but have always found them (as well as all other Friars) fo poorly pufillanimous, as to be thoroughly perfuaded that a man of common courage might drive a dozen of them to the end of the world with a cudgel. Their conftant way of life, as it keeps them at a great diftance from all forts of danger, enervates their minds, and, inftead of enterprife and intrepidity, infufes into them a female fpirit of meek-

meekness and obsequiousness, with a plentiful mixture of dissimulation and hypocrisy. Not one of the many I have known, but partook more or less of this character.

With such a notion of them, produced by many years of observation and reflection, I have read a good many of those books lately written against them with a view to make them all be considered as Conspirators, Traitors, and Regicides by principle and system. But too much of malicious disingenuity is contained in those books. Far from having been convinced by the reasons offered in them, I do not even believe that they have had a hand in the attempt of *D'Aveiro*, for which I can very well account in a simple manner, and without having recourse to marvellous complicated plots. The very proceedings of this Government against them have rivetted my incredulity as to their having partaken in that attempt; nor is it possible

to

to conceive, that a large body of such men as I know them to be, cunning, cautious, and fearful, would enter into a conspiracy headed by a haughty, imprudent, and desperate man such as *D'Aveiro,* and composed of men and women of different ages and conditions; which conspiracy, had it even proved succesful, would still, and at the very best, have left them just where they were and as they were.

But let us grant for argument's sake that some few (or many, if you will) have entered into that conspiracy. Where was the difficulty to hang those few (or many) after a trial not secret, not mysterious, but fair and open to the whole nation? Not one Jesuit has as yet been put to death upon this account, but all have been exported out of the country and banished it for ever, without the least discrimination between the innocent and the guilty; which levelling execution I cannot at all reconcile with my ideas of equity

equity and justice. It is true that old *Malagrida* and two or three more (none of them Portuguese, but all Italians, which is remarkable) have been detained and thrown into jail. They have now been above two years *(a)* in the inquisition. But what has the inquisition to do with regicides, if this government is persuaded that regicides they are? Why have they not been hanged with the Duke *D'Aveiro* and the other conspirators? The power that could easily banish thousands, could as easily hang a dozen or two, or as many as you will. Why was this not done? Who could hinder it? The pope? The people? Some foreign power? No. The whole world would have approved of the punishment inflicted upon convicted regicides. And why is recourse had to the pens of mercenary writers,

(a) *Long after the date of this letter poor Malagrida has been burnt as an Heretick, charged amongst other things of having written while in the prisons of the Inquisition, that the Virgin Mary spoke Latin when still in St. Ann's womb. I know not what is become of his brother regicides.*

and

and so much pains taken to blacken the whole order, when its guilty individuals were completely within the reach of avenging justice? Why are such efforts made *abroad* to make the world believe that they are a set of villains, when *at home* no body is allowed to speak either good or ill of them? That each jesuit is a downright villain, always ready at the nod of his general, his provincial, his rector, or his prefect, to turn traitor, to turn conspirator, to turn King-killer, is an assertion that may be credited by enthusiasts, and by those who hate without knowing why, whose number is larger than vulgar observers are aware of; but never will be credited by men of sober thinking, by men acquainted with the varieties of our tempers and inclinations, by men who have remarked how perfectly impossible it is to bring a vast number of individuals to think and act as one man.

My opinion of the Jesuits' society is therefore this, that they are obnoxious to the great fociety of mankind, not becaufe they are traitors and regicides by principle and fyftem, but becaufe they are indefatigable accumulators of riches which they do not want. Their maintenance requires but little, as they live in community, feed poorly, drefs poorly, and lodge poorly. What need have they to plunder their neighbours with their trade and banking, and hoard up treafures and treafures, when they lead a mean life and cannot by inftitution lead a better? Why are they for ever hunting after inheritances, always (or almoft always) to the prejudice of lawful heirs? What will they do with thofe treafures? Or if they have any good reafon (which is inconceivable) for acting in this manner, why do they not tell it aloud?

Indeed if they are to be annihilated, this avarice of theirs is more than a fufficient motive. But inftead of going this way to work, and call them *Robbers*, which may be done with juftice, as the
desire

defire of robbing is the true and notorious fpirit of their order, great trouble is taken by means of the prefs at *Lucca*, *Venice*, *Lugano*, and other places, to cry them down as *Murtherers*, which in the nature of things cannot be the fpirit of a large body.

Befides the fpirit of robbing, there is that of domineering, which might have been an article of accufation againft them. This is another of their true and notorious characterifticks, that has long made them odious to all men of fenfe and probity. What need have they of influence and authority in the ftates where they are eftablifhed, and even in the ftates where they have no eftablifhment at all; that is, in thofe countries, which we, perhaps with too much acrimony, call heretical? How are influence and authority in any ftate to be reconciled with that profeffion which obliges them to eat, drefs, and lodge poorly, as I faid, and to tread in the footfteps of HIM whofe *companions they*

they call themselves? Why do they ever shun the houses of the poor, where religious men ought always to be assisting and comforting? And what business have they in the palaces of the great, where they are perpetually intruding? What are they doing in the courts of princes, where they are incessantly endeavouring to get a greater and greater footing? Many and many times has my indignation been raised to see them there, smiling, bowing, whispering, fawning, caballing, and intriguing ten thousand times more than the meanest courtiers.

But of these and other matters *Ragionerem più adagio insieme poi*, as the Evangelist said to *Astolfo*. Mean while, as the hour of departure is approaching, I have employed yesterday and to-day in visiting over again and a-foot the ruins of this metropolis, and those many clusters of habitations, which have been built for the reception of those unfortunate creatures whom the earthquake has bereft of their homes.

Of thofe ruins I have already tried to give you fome idea: but I muft again recommend to you not to forget when you read that defcription, that words cannot come up to fo vaft a fcene of horrible defolation.

By comparing the topography of thefe ruins (both in the town and country) with a map of Portugal, it appears that the main force of that memorable concuffion was collected in a narrow line from Eaft to Weft; and that the chief mifchief caufed by it, fell upon thofe buildings that happened to lie along that line: fo that it was not the folidity of its walls that faved the great edifice at *Mafra* from deftruction, but its being at fome diftance from the courfe of the motion. Had this not been the cafe, that edifice could never have efcaped the violence which fhattered the ftony fides of the high hill near *Cintra*, and made fome of
its

its cliffs roll down into the fubjacent plain.

When the fury of the earthquake fubfided, and the univerfal diftraction was in fome meafure appeafed, the inhabitants of *Lifbon* haftened to raife all about the neighbouring hills fuch temporary walls and roofs, as could immediately fcreen them from the fevere weather that fucceeded the immenfe calamity, and have progreffively built feveral fmall villages compofed of fmall houfes and cottages, fome of wood and fome of brick, which are very pretty to look at, as they are regularly difpofed, and as it is the general cuftom here to whitewafh the outfide of all their dwellings.

Thofe fmall houfes and cottages they call *Barraca's:* a very proper appellation, as this word, which has got admiffion in almoft all the languages of Europe, means in them all *A very fmall habitation for man.*

In crossing those parts of the town which have not been demolished, it was impossible not to take notice of the nastiness of the streets. The abominable stink and the vast heaps that cause it, render many of those streets impassable. I am told that there are rigid laws against the infamous practice of throwing any filth down the windows: but what are laws when there is no power to enforce their execution?

One of the things that most surprise a stranger as he rambles about this town, is that great number of Negroes who swarm in every corner.

Many of these unhappy wretches are natives of Africa, and many born of African parents either in Portugal or in its ultramarine dominions. No ship comes from those regions without bringing some of either sex; and, when they are here, they are allowed to marry not only among themselves, but also with those of a different colour. These cross-marriages have

Vol. I.   T   filled

filled the country with different breeds of human monsters. A black and a white produce a *mulatto*. Then a mulatto joins with a black or a white, and two other creatures are engendered, both called *mestices*. Then the *mestices white* join with the *mestices black*, or with true blacks, true white, or mulattos; and all branch out into so many and various kinds, that it becomes very difficult, if not impossible, to distinguish them by peculiar names, though they are all discriminated by their peculiar hues.

To such a degree the original breed is here depraved, that to be *a Blanco*; that is, *a perfect white*, is become a title of honour: so that when a Portuguese says that he is *a Blanco*, you are not to understand that he is *a white man*, which is the real signification of the word; but that he is an honest man, a man of honour, a man of family, a man of consequence and importance.

To

To all these mongrel mixtures you may add the Jewish. Portugal abounds with Jews who personate Christians, and often intermarry both with the white and the other generations. You will easily comprehend that this cannot much contribute towards the farther improvement of those genealogies which make so good a figure on the shelves of the library at *Mafra*.

These strange combinations have filled this town with such a variety of odd faces, as to make the traveller doubt whether *Lisbon* is in Europe; and it may be foreseen, that in a few centuries not a drop of pure Portuguese blood will be left here, but all will be corrupted between Jews and Negroes, notwithstanding their most holy tribunal of the sacred inquisition.

To obviate one of the two evils (which might both be removed by a secular tribunal) the inquisition is always upon the watch to discover the Jews; and when any

any is found out, you know how he is treated. Tell an inquifitor that you are a Jew becaufe it has pleafed God to make you a Jew, and that you do not think yourfelf entitled to undo what God has done, the good Father will throw you into the fire as fure as if you were a chip.

But as one evil breeds another, the inceffant diligence of the inquifition to detect the Jews, makes them redouble their arts of concealment, and (what completes the bleffing) multiplies fuperftition and encreafes hypocrify. Hence it happens that numbers of both fexes, and of all ages and conditions, go about with long rofaries between their thumb and fingers, muttering *paters* and *aves*, that they may be deemed Chriftians if they are Jews, or not be miftaken for Jews if they are Chriftians.

How the Jews can bear to live amidft inceffant danger, is utterly inconceivable. There is a ftubborn perverfenefs in their defying the law of Portugal that almoft

juftifies

justifies the inquisitorial rage. Would you not fly into a passion and roll down-stairs the impudent fellow who was resolved to stay in your own house in spight of your teeth?

In my long walk of yesterday and to-day, I have entered a good number of artists' shops, and found to my no small surprise that they belong mostly to strangers. One would be apt to suspect that the industry of this nation is not great; and the suspicion will increase, when you are told that linen, woollen-cloth, silk-stuffs, and almost all other productions of the loom, are by the Portuguese imported from abroad, though they have at home many of the materials. This is also the case with regard to all sorts of steel, copper, and brass-work, except what is used in mean houses; that is, what does not require much perfection of workmanship. Would you believe that even their shoes they procure from England and from France? I am told that the few who will have shoes made on purpose for their own feet, must apply to the few foreign shoemakers scattered about this town, and submit to pay exhorbitant prices. Even taylors are foreigners for the greatest part; at least those who are most in vogue; and as to French barbers and hair-dressers, they swarm here as well as in England. Statuaries, architects, and engravers they never had of any note. As to painters they can boast but of one, *Alonzo Sanchez Coello*, a disciple of our great *Raphael*, and a favourite of Philip II. who used to call him *Titian the second*. He was employed by that King in the *Escurial*, which he contributed to adorn. His name is more known to the Italians than to the Portuguese.

I will not omit to say that I wanted a plan of this town to help myself in my excursions; but was assured that such a thing had never been thought on, though considering its extent and the great resort of strangers, one would think that many

by

by the probability of profit might be tempted to make it.

To range about such a wide scene of curiosity as this metropolis and its neighbourhood, gives certainly much satisfaction to an inquisitive pair of eyes. But if my eyes are pleased, my ears pay for it by a torment peculiar to the country, which I have suffered every day since my arrival, holidays excepted.

This torment is caused by the creaking of the cart-wheels. I question whether the stink of the dirtiest streets is not more supportable to the nostrils than that shrillness to the ears. The cart-wheels here are made out of two boards nailed together, and clumsily cut in a circular form. Yet the painful noise they make might be obviated, would carmen but grease their axles: but they say that the devil would then do mischief to their oxen, and that noise frightens him away. Did you ever hear a better reason for sparing grease? *Saavedra* in his *Don Quixote*, takes

takes notice of his countrymen's opinion about the noise of cart-wheels, "*de cuyo chirrio aspero y continuado se dize che huyen los lobos y los ossos,*" by whose grating and incessant shrillness they say that wolves and bears are put to flight. If this Spanish notion is not warranted by experience, probability will render it excusable: but the Portuguese have still higher expectations from the noise of a cart-wheel.

These and many other observations have as yet given me no great idea of the common sense of this nation; and as I have brought no recommendatory letters to introduce me to the higher class, where I might find something to make me amends for the little pleasure I have in observing the lower, I have resolved to stay no longer here; and I hope that not more than one of my letters will be dated from this metropolis.

I will conclude this with an exclamation made by an Italian friend of mine

on

on his landing here after an absence like mine from his native country. *Quanti preti! Quanti frati! Quanti Muli!*

LETTER XXXII.

An important dialogue. Parade of Knowledge. Jesuits way of teaching.

Lisbon, Sept. 16. 1760.

I Quit Lisbon to-morrow. My passports are dispatched, and I have just signed the bargain with the *Calesciros* who are to carry me to Madrid in fifteen days. I take Batiste with me. My farewell compliments to the British Ambassador, the English nuns, the Genoese capuchins, and some other people, are all paid, and my things are pack'd up: so that to-morrow-night I shall sleep on the other side of the *Tagus*. Let me now write my last letter from *Lisbon*.

I have already given you to understand, that my opinon of the Portuguese literature is very low; and a few additional observations, which I have had occasion to make this morning on this subject, have not heighten'd that opinion. But before I give you those observations, let me translate a *Dialogue* out of a Portuguese book.

QUESTION. *Don Joseph the first, whose son is he?*

ANSWER. *Of King John V, and Queen Maria Anna of Austria.*

QU. *In what year was he born?*
ANS. *In* 1714.
QU. *On what day?*
ANS. *The sixth of June.*
QU. *When and by whom was he baptized?*
ANS. *Aug.* 29, *of the same year by Cardinal de Cugna.*
QU. *Whom has he married?*
ANS. *Being still Prince of Brasil, he married the most serene Infanta of Spain Dona Mariana Victoria.*
QU. *Who brought about this marriage?*
ANS.

Ans. *Antony Guedes de Pereira while he was envoy at the court of Madrid.*

Qu. *Who went to fetch in due form the most serene lady Infanta?*

Ans. *Dom Rodrigo Eanes de Sà Marquis of Abrantes.*

Qu. *When did this Lady reach Portugal?*

Ans. *On January 19, 1729.*

Qu. *When did she enter Lisbon?*

Ans. *On Feb. 12, of the same year.*

Qu. *When did King Joseph the First begin to reign?*

Ans. *On the last of July 1750.*

Qu. *When was he proclaimed?*

Ans. *On Sept. 7. of the same year.*

Qu. *How many children has he?*

Ans. *He has four daughters, who are the Lady Princess of Brasil Dona Maria Frances Isabel; the Lady Infanta Dona Maria Anna Frances; the Lady Infanta Dona Maria Frances Dorothy; and the Lady Infanta Dona Maria Frances Benedicta.*

And

And with this fine Dialogue ends a Portuguese book printed in 1750, intitled *Inſtruçaõ de Principiantes*, &c. that is, " *An Inſtruction to Beginners, and a* " *new Method by which the firſt Letters* " *are to be learned, for the Uſe of Schools,*" &c.

This book was composed by the profeſſors of the royal ſchool which goes by the name of *As Eſcolas de Noſſa Senhora das Neceſſidades*; that is, *The Schools of our Lady of the Neceſſities*; to which ſchools (or ſchool) the Portugueſe parents who intend to give a liberal education to their children, muſt ſend them, as no other ſchool is here permitted either public or private.

Soon after my arrival I inquired whether in *Liſbon* there was an univerſity; and was informed that theſe ſchools were here in the ſtead of an univerſity. Being deſirous to form ſome acquaintance with the profeſſors there, I ſent (directed for

the

the heads of the schools) a large sheet of ancient Greek characters, collected and methodically disposed by a very learned Englishman called *Morton*, and published in London not long before my departure.

The sheet was accompanied with as civil a letter as I could possibly put together; and it proved an agreeable present, if I am to believe two of those professors who came to me three days after, to return me thanks in their own and their collegues' name.

You may well think that I received them with very submissive civility, and my respect prevailed upon them to stay dinner with me. During a good part of the afternoon they prattled with a volubility, which (as far as I have observed) is characteristical to the Portuguese. It was pretty visible that they both wanted to impose themselves upon me for mighty learned men, and to make me conceive a great opinion of their schools, of their country, and of themselves. However, their learning seem'd to me not great, and their manner of conveying it by much too pompous. Their discourse was plentifully larded with such Latin sentences as are in every school-boy's mouth, and the names of *Tully* and *Virgil* graced too many of their periods. They had some distant glimmering of the French literature, and had heard the names of Moliere and Boileau; but with regard to that of Italy and of England, neither of them knew more than my negro. The sheet of Greek alphabets, which I had sent them, is hung up, they said, in one of their schools; but they honestly own'd that none of them meddled much with Greek.

My patience was nearly worn out when they left me, fully persuaded I suppose, that they had amazed me with the variety of their knowledge and the fluency of their elocution. Hearing that these were two of the chief professors *das Necesf-*

ceſſitades, I found means to return the visit when I was sure of not finding them at home, and thought no further about them. However this morning they called on me again, on purpose to thank me again, as they said, for my present, which had been examined by their collegues, and found to be *huma valeroza compoſiçaõ (a noble compoſition)*, and as they had taken notice of my sollicitude to inform myself of whatever was relative to their schools, they desired my acceptance of the book, out of which I have extracted the above dialogue, assuring me that it was one of the most elegant and learned *compoſiçaõms* in their language.

They were no sooner gone than I fell to reading it. It is divided into two parts nearly equal. The first is a most jejune abridgment of their history, from count *Dom Henrico* of Burgundy (who liv'd in the eleventh century) down to the present reign inclusively. The second part

is

is no more than the same abridgment thrown into dialogues, of which I have given you the laſt. The ſtyle of theſe is plain, becauſe no art could make it otherwiſe; but as for that of the hiſtory (or abridgment) there are few things more thickly ſown with over-ſtrained thoughts and puerile conceits.

By the title I had miſtaken it for a new-year's-gift to a child; yet I ſee by the preface, that they put it into the hands of thoſe young men who from the ſchool of humanity are advanced to that of rhetorick. How it can contribute to make young men rhetoricians, is beyond my comprehenſion; and if you review my faithful tranſlation of the dialogue, you will agree with me, that ſuch trifles ought to have been taught in the nurſery, and not in a royal ſchool of rhetorick. *Kelly's* boys, who are pupils to the younger of my viſitors, have told me, that this and their other ſchool-books muſt be learned by heart in each

re-

respective school; for such is the method: and the scholars who neglect to commit their daily lessons to memory, are sure of punishment.

What I have further to remark on this subject is, that *as Escolas das Necessidades* is a Philippine convent, and of course the professors are Philippine friars. The Jesuits were formerly possessed of the exclusive privilege of teaching the youth of *Lisbon*; but soon after their expulsion this honour was conferred by the government upon the Philippines; and I am much mistaken if the poor lads are not fallen from the frying-pan into the fire.

It is a positive fact that in Italy the Jesuits have endeavoured to root out all literature. Before the institution of their order we had such a number of men eminent in various branches of science, from (*a*) Dante down to (*b*) Galileo, as few,

---

(*a*) Dante *was born in* 1265.
(*b*) Galileo *died in* 1642.

if any, of the modern nations can show. But as soon as the Jesuits got possession of our schools under the pretence of teaching our youth *gratis*, there was almost an end amongst us of historians, politicians, philosophers, and poets. The Jesuits began by discrediting the Greek tongue, and persuaded us that it was unnecessary. Then by means of their voluminous Latin grammars they rendered the acquisition of the Latin next to impossible, as it is almost impossible to learn a thing unknown by means of a thing equally unknown. They corrupted even our language, and caused such a deluge of equivocal wit to be poured over our writings of all kinds, that during their reign, that is, during the last century, we excited the ridicule of the neighbouring nations, in whom long before we had raised astonishment.

It was luckily for us that the Jesuits could never obtain admission into the university of Pisa, and that they were

not

not even allowed to teach in the inferior schools of Tuscany; so that it was at last in the power of the Tuscans and of *Galileo*'s disciples and followers, to rescue us from barbarity, and restore the learning of Italy to purity and splendour. *Rinaldini, Aggiunti,* the two *Del Buono's, Viviani, Bellini, Torricelli, Redi,* and several other men, deliver'd us in a good measure from our false instructors; false with regard to us, though not to themselves, as they taught each other very well, and were themselves almost the only men of science throughout the country.

And here it may not be amiss to record, that amongst our Italian princes, it was our glorious king *Victor Amadeus* who first detected the deep-laid schemes of the Jesuits, and who first had the courage to strip them throughout his dominions of the exclusive privilege of teaching us. And it is originally to him that the greater part of the Italian states owe the great blessing of having at present but a very few Jesuits for teachers.

In this country, however, it was not very judicious to substitute the Philippines to the Jesuits, if the Philippines are for ignorance like those of Italy, as I am persuaded they are. But it is to be hoped that these reverend fathers have been only temporarily entrusted with this important charge, until the present disturbances are somewhat quieted. I am told, that this government intends to put the public schools into better regulations, and that a good number of truly learned men are soon to be procured from other countries: nay, I am positively assured, that old *Facciolati* the philologist, father *Frisi* the mathematician, and some other eminent men from Padua, Milan, and other parts of Italy, are expected to be soon here; that a new university is to be instituted in this town, into which some of the *Cohimbra*-professors are to be incorporated, and that ancient university totally suppressed. How

How much of truth there is in these reports, I have not been able to ascertain. Perhaps the day approaches, that the Portuguese will emerge from ignorance and superstition, and come up to a level with some other Catholic nations.

LETTER XXXIII.

Fleas, rats, and other conveniencies. Love in one place and liberty in another. Devotion here and devotion there.

Aldeagallega, Sept. 17, 1760.

THE poor traveller has quitted Lisbon to-day in the afternoon, in order to journey on to his native land.

The river *Tagus*, not three miles broad at the mouth, is full nine miles where I crossed it to-day: but the wind proved so favourable, that in about three hours I sailed over it in an open boat.

And here I am in the best inn *(Estallage* they call it here) of *Aldeagallega*. My apartment is nothing more than a large

large room hung all round with fine broad cobwebs, and furnifhed with a narrow mat for its inhabitant to ftretch his limbs upon, whenever he fhall wifh to go to fleep. Glafs-windows this room has none; but inftead of panes there are fhutters fo full of chinks, that all the children of Eolus may pafs them. As for a bed, tables, chairs, pictures, and other things in ufe amongft Chriftians and Mahometans, here are none; and through the various clefts of the boards which form this floor, I expect that a multitude of rats will come out to-night to peep at me, and eat me perhaps, as the *Eftallageiro* has no victuals either for them or for any body elfe.

Such is the lodging I have got for to-night. But although the danger from the rats may be rather imaginary than real, yet it is evident that I fhall not efcape with a whole fkin from the fleas, which run on all fides of this room in numerous fquadrons, and feem impatiently

tiently to wait for my putting out the light that they may come and eat me.

However, upon this mat I shall not sleep. Batiste, who has travell'd much up and down this country, has bought me a large bag, which is to serve me instead of a bed as long as my journey through Portugal will last; and he is this minute come to tell me, that he has found dry straw sufficient to fill it; so that he is sure I shall pass a comfortable night upon it, with the help of the sheets and coverlet that he has likewise provided. As to food, we have brought with us fowls, hams, sausages, pies, cakes, and cheese; therefore neither of us shall meet with the dismal fate of *Jugurtha* after he fell into the hands of the merciless Romans.

And now, ye Queens of Parnassus, as a reward for my long past services, for which you never paid me, I beseech you to obtain from your friend Apollo, that to-morrow he be so kind as to bring day over this region betimes, that I may early see the way which leads travellers from the most paltry inn of *Aldeagallega*.

A Postscript.

Supper being over, and finding in myself an invincible reluctance to fall down upon the straw-bag, I went to take a short walk. The air is quite soft and calm, and the moon shines bright. As I was moving on with weary steps and busy imagination, I found myself by the side of the *Tagus*, which is within pistol-shot of the *Estallage*. There I saw many a happy couple, some sitting on the bank, some walking backwards and forwards, all whispering, all hugging, all enjoying each other in the cool of the evening.

Good folks! said I to myself. What sort of supper they have had I know not, and probably their beds are no better than that which Batiste has provided for me! And yet they are happy in each other's other's kindnefs. Why do the Englifh ftun foreigners with their liberty? Is it not liberty to wander by the river-fide at *Aldeagallega*, telling a gentle maid whatever comes uppermoft, without a thought of miniftry, politics, or faction?

Happy *Aldeagallegans!* go on in this way for ever, and never think nor enquire how the money of the nation is fpent!

I had already taken notice that the Portuguefe are of a difpofition much more amorous than the Englifh, and waited for an opportunity to tell you fo. The inhabitants of this village walking thus lovingly *chacun avec fa chacune* have now given me that opportunity. But this is generally the cafe with all nations in warm climates. The natives of a cold region can fcarcely have right notions of the effect of a warm temperature. In northern latitudes a good deal of cloathing and firing is required to pafs life away with fome comfort; and where cloathing and firing are much wanting, much

thought

thought and much time muſt be ſpent to procure them. The caſe is ſomewhat different in thoſe countries where fewer things are neceſſary to life. This is the reaſon why in England there are multitudes who have ſcarcely been in love once in their lives. Many a debauchee have I ſeen in England during ten years, but very ſeldom a true *innamorato*. In Portugal all are in love from the day of their nativity to that of their deceaſe, and *Camoens* knew what he was about when he ſaid

Venus bella
Affeyçoada a gente Luſitana.
" *Fair Venus cheriſhes the Portugueſe.*"

Love is the predominant paſſion on the *Tagus*, as *Liberty* on the *Thames*.

There are many more ſtriking differences between the Portugueſe and the Engliſh; but that amongſt other which is moſt remarkable, is their different way of being devout, when by devotion we mean the outward ſhow of religion, independent

dent of its spirit. See the English at church. They sit or stand with a composed look; sing their psalms and anthems with an even tone of voice; and not one in a hundred betrays the least enthusiasm, except a few of those two sects called *Methodists* and *Quakers*, who might be termed the Lusitanick part of the British nation.

The Portuguese on the contrary when at church, are devout to a superlative degree. They are almost all the time upon their knees; raise their eyes wistfully up, fix the fingers of one hand closely between those of the other; sing very loud, or utter ejaculations with great earnestness, and often strike their breasts with their hands. Leave their churches and look at their houses. You will see many crosses painted on their outward walls, or a Madona, or a St. Francis, or a St. Anthony. Look at one of their friars coming in. Men, women, and children will hastily get up, run to him, and humbly

humbly kifs his hand, or his sleeve, or the hem of his garment, or the beads that hang from his waist. Every evening you see them in numbers kneeling round a high crucifix planted in the middle of a street, singing litanies with their utmost power of voice. Then none of them dares to die without going through many preparatory rites, which is not the case in England: and when they are dead, they are buried dress'd up in a habit that must be bought of a Franciscan or a Dominican Friar, of whose sanctity they had a good opinion. I remember an impudent Portuguese Franciscan I met once in a boat as I was going down our *Po*, who looked upon all Italians as little less than hereticks. What led him into this opinion was, that no body in Italy would give him a farthing for his coat, which in Portugal, he could sell at will for forty or fifty crowns.

What words can express the devotion of the Portuguese to the Virgin Mary?

The

The southern Italians scarcely rate her so high as the Portuguese: but the English never think of her. You may easily imagine that those who make nothing of the Virgin, make less than nothing of the Saints, which is not the case either in Italy or in Portugal. Yet the Portuguese revere them a great deal more than we do; and above all you cannot conceive what sublime notions they have of St. Anthony! The twelve apostles all together have not the hundredth part of the prayers directed to them that are to him. St. Anthony was a countryman of theirs; and as such, they take it for granted that he will mind them more than any of the apostles or any other. But what business have they with St. Francis, who was our countryman, and, I think, never visited Portugal in his life? Yet they put him upon a level with their own St. Francis, and even a degree higher, if we may judge by their *Francisco's* and *Francisca's*, who are much more numerous throughout

their

their country than the *Antonio's* and *Antonia's*. You may have a specimen of the Portuguese fondness, first for our Lady, and then for St. Francis, if you will look back again to the dialogue out of the Philippine-book. There you will find that each of the King's four daughters was christened by the name of *Mary Frances*.

But the great devotion of the Portuguese does not interfere at all with their love of the other sex, or their love of dancing, which is another of their mighty loves. As soon as they have done with evening-singing of litanies before their crucifixes in the streets, and at their windows or balconies, if you take a ramble about the streets, you see in houses and shops numbers of them dancing merrily at the sound of a guittar or two, while some of the company, or the guittarists themselves, sing a song to the tune. None of your *minuets* and your *aimables*. Their dances are not of such a cold, insipid,

sipid, and frenchified kind. They chiefly consist in jumps and jerks, in languid postures and languid falls, in a quick and incessant striking of their heels on the ground, perfectly calculated to kindle the mind with joy and the heart with desire.

Thus live the Portuguese in an uninterrupted round of devotion and pleasure. They are neither gluttons nor drunkards, though their country wants neither food nor drink. Their beef and veal indeed are not so generally good as in England, or in the western and northern parts of Italy; but their pork, mutton, and lamb are excellent; and so are their chickens, fowls, ducks, turkeys, and game. As for fish, the Lisbon-market is perhaps the most plentifully and most variously supplied in Europe; and all their fruit and garden-stuff is superlatively good. The low people seldom taste flesh; but the best sort keep very good tables and have French cooks. To keep a table, however, must require a considerable expence in Lisbon, if to live at home costs proportionably as much as to live at an inn. My table at Kelly's, which was far from being a sumptuous one, cost me above a guinea a day. But I know nothing as to the manner of living of the great in Lisbon, because I have seen none. By what I have seen of the inferior classes, they seem to like a good house, if they have one that is good: but if they have it not, a *Baracca* will do quite as well. As to houshold furniture they have no refined ideas. A hard matrafs in a corner, or a mat, or their own cloaths, will stand them in stead of as good beds as down can make; for which reason they look generally dirty. Almost any thing with them will supply the place of victuals; and water is excellent to quench the thirst, especially such good water as they have here.

Thus live the Portuguese, without thinking much of to-morrow; that plaguy *to-morrow,* which, along with
liberty,

liberty, is always uppermost in the head of an Englishman. In general they are healthy and full of spirits, and live long, if we may judge by the great number of old people that one sees in their metropolis. Whether the proportion of happiness is greater in Portugal than in England, or the contrary, I have no means of calculating; but the Portuguese do not look as if they were disturbed by desire of change, or fear of want.

The ruin of their capital was a misfortune eternally to be commiserated. Speaking of it, the Portuguese would say: *Quem naõ ha visto Lisboa, naõ ha visto cosa boa*; "*he who has not seen Lisbon, has seen nothing that is good.*" Of such partial sayings almost every nation has one, if not more. *Quien no ha visto Sevilla, no ha visto maravilla.* "*He who has not seen Seville has not* "*seen a wonder.*" *Qui n' a point vu Versaille, n' a vu rien qui vaille.* "*He who has* "*not seen Versailles has seen nothing worth* "*seeing.*" I could give you many more sayings

sayings of this sort, if I had a mind. That of the Neapolitans is the most energetick of them all, though not in rhyme. *Vedi Napoli e po' mori.* " *See Naples, and* " *then die.*"

It is now time to end my *Postcript*. I go to lie down on my straw-bag, and set the fleas and rats at defiance.

The END of the FIRST VOLUME.

www.ingramcontent.com/pod-product-compliance
Lightning Source LLC
Chambersburg PA
CBHW030809230426
43667CB00008B/1133